C000178745

The World Domi
Handbook

Rule the World Within a Year
Or Your Money Back*

Cash Peters

with illustrations by Max Ellis

*probably

NEW ENGLISH LIBRARY
Hodder and Stoughton

Copyright © 1990 by Cash Peters
Illustrations copyright © 1990 by
Max Ellis

First published in Great Britain in 1990
by New English Library paperbacks

*A New English Library
paperback original*

The excerpt on p 181 from "If I Ruled
the World" (Ornadel/Bricusse), ©
Delfont Music Limited, reproduced
by permission of Warner Chappell
Music Limited.

British Library C.I.P.
Peters, Cash
  The world domination handbook : rule
  the world within a year or your money
  back.
  I. Title
  828.91409

ISBN 0-450-53224-0

Printed and bound in Great Britain for
Hodder and Stoughton Paperbacks, a
division of Hodder and Stoughton Ltd.,
Mill Road, Dunton Green, Sevenoaks,
Kent TN13 2YA. (Editorial Office: 47
Bedford Square, London, WC1B 3DP)
by Richard Clay Ltd, Bungay, Suffolk.
Typeset by Hewer Text Composition
Services, Edinburgh.

Malcontents

By the same author:

Fear Is A Five-Letter Word
The Sleepy Dell Orphanage Massacre
Thugs in Love
Luscious Lucy Meets the Venture Scouts
Sheepshanks of Desire

By other authors:

A Woman of Substance
Delia Smith's Complete Cookery Course
Five Go To Smuggler's Top
Kane and Abel
Jan – The Story of a Dutch Barge Dog

In*tro*duction

Make no mistake, this book could be highly dangerous in the wrong hands.

For a start, it's quite heavy, so a sudden blow to the face with it could easily knock your front teeth out. But more than that, scattered within its pages you will find specific, detailed instructions for achieving power – Divine Power, global power, power over billions of people. In short, you will learn how to take over the world.

What we have here is history in the making – something you can tell your children and grandchildren in years to come, in the sure and confident knowledge that they won't be the slightest bit interested.

Up to now, maybe you thought you were an insignificant nobody, powerless to influence the course of world affairs. If so, think again! Because with the help of our friends the Abercorn family, we'll demonstrate how simple it is for you to achieve world domination. Just follow the easy-to-read, step-by-step, somewhat-over-hyphenated instructions in this book, and you too could become a spiritual leader and Messiah to virtually the whole of civilisation.

And don't worry about not being the real thing either. *Real* Messiahs are scarcer than Scotsmen on flag-days and, since nobody else is doing anything at the moment, it may as well be you.

Let's face it, global domination is a pretty neat trick if you can pull it off, so why not join forces with us and have a go, starting today? Between us we could topple Communist dictatorships, put the wind up the United Nations and bring NATO to its knees. Together, we will stick our hand up the skirt of parliamentary government and tweak the very buttocks of Democracy 'til she squeals for mercy.

Now before we go on, any questions . . . ?

1

Q: *Hello!*

Yes – the gentleman over there, carrying a big Q.

Q: *But surely, I can't conquer the world alone, can I? I'm not
Bob Soddin' Geldof! I'm only little old me. Existing world
leaders will never take me seriously.*

Good point.

But don't forget that world leaders are really no different to
you or me. They have their weaknesses just as we all do, the
same moments of self-doubt, the same annoying hiccups in
their daily life – I mean, the ball is just as capable of jamming
on Mikhail Gorbachev's deodorant as it is on yours. And
Lech Walesa could easily stub his toe while Hoovering or spill
damson jam down his best sports-jacket, in exactly the same
way that you or I can. They are only human after all – nothing
special. So don't be overawed by them.

One other point worth bearing in mind, too, is that when
we say 'take over the world', we don't actually mean the
whole planet. After all, around 70% of the earth is underwater, and if you look at the remaining 30%, over a third of
that is arable land and pasture, 24% is forest, 33% is covered
by buildings, and the rest is owned by some Arab whose name
I forget for the moment. In other words, the area of the earth
you're going to have to take control of is really quite tiny, so
don't be discouraged. Be patient – follow these instructions to
the letter and success will surely follow. Remember, Hiro-
shima wasn't rebuilt in a day.

And anyway, you only have to take one look at all the
egotists, shysters, bullies and windbags in power right now to
see that, no matter who you are, you're definitely in with a
chance!

Q. *Yes, but I'll need* millions *of people to support me, won't I?
Not just one or two. This World Domination lark is bloody
hopeless!*

Look, if you really can't sleep at nights for worrying about
who will support you and who won't, you obviously don't
understand human behaviour at all.

The world is full of sheep. Millions and millions of people

2

all doing the same things, thinking the same thoughts, behaving in the same way, and so on. Sheep enjoy habit and routine. They are lazy. They like to be ordered about, told what to do and what to buy. Not only that, but they like to do and buy what everyone else is doing and buying. How else could you explain the way completely duff products sell by the million in this country, and why feeble whacko political causes engage such a nationwide following?

Who do you suppose buys all those nasty little teddy bears in Beefeater uniforms you find on sale at British airports? And what kind of people would have a big fluffy Garfield spreadeagled across their car-window? Or a sticker saying 'Dyslexics Do It With Frixo Ktik Yipwifu'? And who gets stuck on the southbound carriageway of the M1 every Bank Holiday Monday because they all set off from home at the same time?

The Masses, that's who!

Again, you only have to think of those gigantic rallies held in Hyde Park on Sunday afternoons by obscure pressure groups with absurd names, such as 'Sofabed Upholsterers Against Trident' or 'Schizophrenics For, and Against, the Bomb'. Who *are* these people, and where do they come from? Nobody knows, but they still come – they can't stop themselves. They're sheep.

Mind you, this doesn't include you and me, does it? Of course not. We're individuals, free-thinking and intelligent, making decisions for ourselves in a considered way. We don't toe the line or conform or fall in with the crowd, do we? Not us. We're special. And that is precisely why you and I together can put this Global Domination Plan into operation, and why everybody else, the sheep, will follow us when we do. Trust me, they will.

Now, perhaps we could have one last readers' question before I introduce you to the Abercorns . . . ?

Q: *Yes, over here . . .*

Thank you, Sir, but I think we should give somebody else a chance. Has anyone besides the man with the big Q got a question . . . ?

. . . Nobody?

Oh, alright, what is it?

Q: *Well, it's all fine and dandy saying that we're going to take over the world, but what if the world doesn't want to be taken over? What if the Superpowers or the Libyans or billions of people in other countries don't agree with us? They might resist, mightn't they? I'm not saying they will, but if they did, wouldn't we get hurt? I mean, look at Gandhi and Jesus Christ. And what about Jane Fonda?*

Sadly, it is a bizarre truth about the human race, that anyone who comes up with a rave idea for altering the status quo, and who proposes peace, love, an end to violence, and co-operation between all races, is immediately considered a threat to civilisation and either nailed to a plank of wood and left there, or at the very least tortured until he agrees to retract what he said about changing things and admits that life is just hunky-dory as it is.

You see, democracy is a fr . . . incidentally, what *about* Jane Fonda?

Q: Sorry. Not Jane Fonda, I mean Martin Luther King.

Oh, right.

You see, democracy is a fragile creature – it depends on all of us mucking in together to nurture it and care for it and keep it alive, otherwise it quickly crumples up and dies.

Which is why so many official agencies exist to remind us of our responsibilities and to make sure we know our place within society and conform. Conformity breeds stability, and democracy needs constant stability in order to survive. It's that old '1984'/Big Brother stuff all over again. That is why council or other government buildings are always the largest structures in any town, to remind us who is Boss. And why parking restrictions seem to be absolutely bloody everywhere these days. It's got little or nothing to do with traffic congestion, that's for sure. Yellow lines along the kerb are simply an unconscious reminder to the man in the street that someone else is in charge and not him.

6

To grasp this, you need to understand a little about the way society is structured.

Put simply, the world is owned by men in blue suits;
run by men in grey suits;
administered by men in brown suits;
maintained by men in boiler suits; and
occupied by men who can't afford suits.

Contrary to what you probably believe, your life is not your own. Whether you live or die, eat or starve, pay your bills or go bust – none of this is up to you. You might think it is, but it isn't.

The government never asks you what you think the tax rate should be, or by how much your mortgage interest should rise. They just fix them and expect you to pay without question. Nor do you have any say about the chemicals they put in the food you eat, the water you drink, or the pollution in the air you breathe, or even the huge amounts of shit they're constantly pumping into our rivers and seas. The future of wildlife, the countryside, in fact the entire human race, is out of your hands. Responsibility for our lives has been handed over to some anonymous, grey little men in grey little suits, sitting in some grey little office somewhere, who have never even heard of us. If you didn't know who they were, you'd walk past them in the street. On the other hand, if you did know who they were, you'd *run* past them in the street.

We're under the thumb, all of us. We have to be, simply because if we weren't, 'normal' life as we know it would disintegrate and there would be none of that vital stability which the countless millions of sheep crave so deeply.

But that is only the start of it. If a sizeable chunk of society should decide to revolt tomorrow, to opt out of conventional living and buck the System by refusing to play the game, whether in a minor way, by defiantly parking wherever, whenever and however they chose; or else by going on indefinite strike, or indulging in unfettered sexual activity in banks and post offices and other places of public recreation, then the status quo would be threatened immediately and democracy undermined. Very soon, the Authorities would get mighty pissed off. They'd send in the army and the riot police; countless arrests would be made, sentences passed, fines exacted, rebels jailed and so on, until such time as the revolt died down, stability was restored and the status quo reigned once more.

And yet it is within the power of ordinary people to do this. The officials in charge are only where they are because we, the citizens of this country, allow them to be. And because we outnumber them by tens of thousands to one, if we did decide that we'd had enough and wanted to change things, we could, and they would be powerless to stop us. We are many, they are few!

The truth is, we have reached a point in history where one guy, if he is determined enough and is backed by the right combination of know-how, personnel and equipment, could take over the world. There is an uprising just waiting to happen here, a rebellion in repose.

What you have in your hands (and I'm assuming it's this book!), is a blueprint for mobilising the Masses, the sheep, the Silent Majority, whatever you want to call them, into action. Many of the plans have already been laid, much of the groundwork is now done. All that is required of you is that you follow the Abercorns' instructions through to their conclusion until you make this World Domination blueprint a reality.

If you are still in doubt about whether to become involved, whether to give up the cosy passive existence you are used to in order to become a rebel and a maverick, then try looking at it another way.

Imagine that the phone rings one day during dinner. You pick it up and it's Steven Spielberg on the line from Hollywood. So, of course, you agree to pay for the call, and in the course of the conversation he says that he's planning to make a movie of your life-story, based on everything that has happened to you so far – your achievements, the hard times, your successes and loves and prosperity – everything.

8

What would you say?

Would you tell him no, it's not possible? That there is nothing to make a movie about? That you have always lived a sort of average, cushy, conventional, nine-to-five existence with few thrills or adventures to speak of? That you were always a bit of a sheep anyway, a conformist, some kind of saintly saccharine goody-two-shoes who never broke the rules, never stood up for what he believed in, never made his or her mark on society? That, yes, it's true you were once given the chance to do something quite extraordinary which involved rising up and taking over the world, but it seemed like too much effort at the time, a wee bit dangerous, and you didn't think you were up to it anyway, so you gave it a miss? Or would you be able to sell him the exclusive world rights to your story, knowing that you were prepared to stand up and be counted with the rest of us?

I think I've made my point, so I'll say no more . . . save that, as you read this book, whenever moments of self-doubt creep in, as they surely will, and you begin questioning the sanity of the whole idea, then that is the time to think of the movie! Think of your name on the list of credits: will it be right up there, sitting proudly above the title where it really belongs, or will it be somewhere towards the bottom of the cast list, buried in amongst the bit-parts and the walk-ons?

Think of all that, and then decide for yourself what to tell Steven when he calls.

Right, any other points . . . ?

Q: *Yes – here!*

No thank you!!

Q: *If we're going to do this properly, why bother trying to mobilise billions of people around the world? Why don't we just get an army together and a few missiles and simply nuke everybody? It would be much cheaper and far less bother.*

You stupid man!

You'll never conquer the world by bombing it, or by massacring whole civilisations indiscriminately, or by

9

terrorising them. Genocide may seem like a neat wheeze in theory, but it is so predictable. Try it, and you'll soon find that The Men In Grey Suits are ready and waiting for you to hit the button. They expect you to do something like that, and so they have special contingency plans drawn up to deal with just such an eventuality. No, I'm afraid that is not the way to win.

You must do it peacefully, without violence, and without harm physically, emotionally or psychologically to any living soul.

Q: *But that takes all the fun out of it! You're crazy.*

Maybe. We'll have to see, won't we?

Anyway, I trust that I've dealt with everything now, so perhaps we can meet the Abercorn family and get on with the book. Any further questions you may have as we go, please don't hesitate to ask.

Thank you.

1

Hey, Let's Meet the Abercorns!

Key Personnel Profile 1: Jeff Abercorn

Jeff started out in life as an actor.

After graduating from the Royal Academy for the Performing Arts and Acting in 1974, he kicked around in the provincial theatre for a while, playing Alexander to Edith Evans' Fanny at Richmond, as well as taking on various minor Shakespearean roles, including Portfolio in *The Merchant of Venice* at Stratford, and Ventaxia in the Amalgamated Union of Engineering Workers' Touring Production of *Twelfth Night*.

For Jeff, like his father before him, the theatre was in his blood,[1] and he was looking forward to a lifetime in the profession. Unfortunately, as it turned out, his acting career was shorter than the shelf-life of a banana, and so, when the work finally dried up, he was forced to enrol with one of London's top modelling agencies where he made a living posing for the illustrations in do-it-yourself manuals.

After appearing in a number of D-I-Y classics, including *Your Twelve Toughest Grouting Problems Solved*[2] and *Flush Joey Away!* (*The Budgie-Disposal Handbook*), Jeff discovered he had quite a flair for the work, thanks to his uncanny resemblance to a simple line drawing, and his unique ability to look completely two-dimensional in any light.

'Flush Joey away!'

[1] Frankie Abercorn was a well-known music hall entertainer in the 1930s, touring the Northern theatres with his sister's inflammable dog act 'Zelda and her Combustible Corgis', before appearing in a number of cheap and forgettable British B-movies. His performance as Jessie Matthews in the 1954 film *The Bucktoothed Chanteuse* was branded 'Unconvincing' by the *Abergavenny Evening Herald*.

[2] Soon to be a major motion picture.

In 1987, with his royalties from *Your Next Twelve Toughest Grouting Problems Solved As Well*, he bought 17, Campbell Avenue, a spacious detached house on the outskirts of a small coastal town in Hampshire called Witchester. Between jobs, he managed to construct his own nuclear shelter in the back garden. Christened 'Sea View', it's a sort of subterranean bungalow twelve feet down, which will serve as both family home and safe haven in the event of, say, the outbreak of thermonuclear war or a surprise raid by Angolan mercenaries on Witchester town centre. In the meantime, however, he uses it to store his expanding collection of novelty home-made wines.

Jeff has been married to Julie for eleven years and they have two children, aged 15 and 12. All have good strong teeth thanks to regular brushing and a balanced healthy diet.

Key Personnel Profile 2: Julie Abercorn

Julie is a busy housewife and mother, although, since the children grew old enough to be neglected, she has been more interested in taking over the world and bringing the government to its knees.

To her mind, despite the ending of Cold War hostilities between East and West, the nuclear threat is ever-present and the attack, when it comes, could be from any one of a dozen loony African or Middle Eastern regimes, with Fiji and New Zealand as rank outsiders. So, with that in mind, she has been busy kitting out the nuclear bunker well in advance of the Big Bang. Actually, it's less of a bunker, more of a buried caravan, but the atmosphere is always snug and welcoming. The curtains are lace, white, chintzy and completely unnecessary since there are no windows; the freezer is well-stocked, and a state-of-the-art TV and video recorder has been installed for the kids, with enough Pixie and Dixie videos to last them through a nuclear winter.

Needless to say, she has already started baking for the Holocaust.

Hobby-wise, Julie is a lifelong fan of sixties' pop sensation The Applejacks and knows everything about them, including a few facts that even The Applejacks themselves aren't sure about. She also has an encyclopaedic knowledge of their chart career that is truly frightening in its accuracy: i.e. 'Tell Me When' – a smash hit in March 1964 – plus 'Like Dreamers Do' and 'Three Little Words' which failed to make the Top Ten. She is also eagerly awaiting the day when The Carpenters get back together again.

As well as her profound fear of Armageddon, Julie nurtures an unshakable belief in the green ethic. She has sworn solemnly to help protect the ozone layer, and vows not to use deodorant or hairspray if ever she visits the Antarctic.

Key Personnel Profile 3: Jeff Abercorn Jnr

The Abercorns have a technical genius for a son!

While still at school, Jeff Jnr began to show a remarkable talent for computer-hacking, when he logged into Witchester town council's database and transferred 70% of their annual budget to the freedom fighters in Nicaragua.

When his letter of expulsion finally came through, he decided to take up illegal computer-entry full-time and has since become expert at breaking into the Pentagon computer in Washington DC, intercepting NATO coded defence commands and infiltrating police data systems worldwide. He was also able to read Douglas Adams' last novel before he'd even posted it to his publishers.

Ever-resourceful and an all-round smart git, Jeff Jnr is quite the inventor. So far, his inventions have included a range of water-resistant vegetables – the most successful of them being the cucumbrella – and something else called 'The Pile Driver', a special seat cover for motorists with haemorrhoids. But his best idea so far has been the world's first truly mobile computer, which fits neatly into a child's push-chair and can be taken anywhere. 'The Pramstrad' has huge potential, but without sufficient backing or resources, he has been unable to market it properly, and so recently took a part-time job selling second-hand sandwiches from a barrow in Witchester market, in the hope of raising enough funds to back the idea himself.

Key Personnel Profile 4: Suzuki Abercorn

At 13, Suzuki is the youngest member of the Abercorn family, and certainly the most Japanese-looking (following a brief affair in the mid-seventies between Julie and the man from the local takeaway), and though taunted mercilessly with all kinds of malicious racial slurs, she takes it all in good part, and hopes to reach the age of 14 without throwing herself off a bridge.

She is growing up to be a sensitive, artistic girl, with an especial interest in anthropology and prehistoric animals. Her bedroom is lined with photographs of different species, from the mighty Brontesistas to the Rogetsthesaurus. Suzuki is currently learning to play the Stylophone – against the express wish of her parents, incidentally, who recently put her down for a course in bomb disposal.

Key Personnel Profile 5: Elsie Greenhalgh, Housekeeper

Meet Mrs Greenhalgh, the Abercorns' robust but lovable West Country housekeeper!

Born and raised in a tiny village on the coast of Southern Cornwall, she moved to Witchester after her husband Ephraim was killed in a freak wine-tasting accident in St Ives.

Though she often tries to suppress it, Mrs Greenhalgh is also a passionate Applejacks fan, which means that she and Julie are never short of things to talk about. However, it often gets overlooked, particularly by the more serious music press, that Elsie was once a performer in her own right, singing backing vocals for fifties' supergroup The Chequestubs, as well as being in the line-up of Kevin Armitage's first and only band Pigswill, before he went on to become a solo artist and, later, a quality greengrocer and florist.

For a brief time, she sang lead vocals for an American jazz combo – Grover Pullover and His Snagged-Sweater Six – and backing tracks on many contemporary titles, such as 'Born Too Young' and 'Everybody's Barmy Bar Me'. Her very last appearance was in 1969, on the top fifty hit 'Give us Yer Wallet, Yer Slimy Bastard!' by The Muggers.

Mrs Greenhalgh has one daughter, Lucette, who, following extensive experiments with the accepted barriers of sexual pigeon-holing, became a full-time lesbian in 1987, purely for financial reasons. It even made the front page of the local paper: 'I already had the haircut, so changing my sexuality was nothing really,' says fun-loving dyke Lucette, 22'.

However, being designated as queer by the news media hasn't halted her progress one jot. Lucette has twelve O-Levels, four A-Levels, a Higher National Diploma in mechanical engineering from the Polytechnic of Central London and a Masters Degree in Divinity from Oxford. She also gained her Doctorate in Philosophy at the University of Bath in 1988. As yet, her career plans are not exactly set in concrete – she currently stacks shelves in Waitrose part-time. But her ambitions are sky-high, and within a year she hopes to work on the bacon-counter.

And there they are – the Abercorns, a typical nuclear family:

Typical nuclear family.

Unfortunately, like many of us today, the Abercorns feel that their lives are not their own, that the world is out of control, hurtling closer and closer towards the Final Holocaust. In spite of the endless propaganda being churned out about improved East–West relations and a safer world, some countries are still producing atomic weapons like there's no tomorrow. Indeed, if they continue producing them, there may well be no tomorrow. Which is why, even now, Jeff and Julie live in fear of that ultimate cataclysm.

Of course, many experts do say that a nuclear winter may not be too different from a British summer, but the Abercorns are taking no chances.

They have thought long and hard about the way things are going, and have concluded that the situation is now much too grave to allow a few faceless bureaucrats in Brussels or Washington or Tripoli or wherever, to screw up the world on our behalf, when we can do it perfectly well for ourselves, thank you very much.

Jeff and Julie feel they have glimpsed the future . . .

Typical post-nuclear family.

. . . and have decided to do something about it.

They hit on the idea of taking over the world about two years ago, and were just waiting for the ammunition to arrive from South Africa, when something else happened: a family emergency that brought everything to a head.

Julie takes up the story:

'It was a Monday night, I remember it well, and we'd been out all evening attending a local Neighbourhood Watch meeting. We didn't arrive home until after 10 o'clock, but when we did, Jeff opened the front door and discovered . . . we'd been burgled!

'It was just terrible. Someone had rifled through my collection of used diaphragms, the kids' bedroom had been daubed with pictures of Tufty and Mr Policeman Badger doing unspeakable things to each other with a tin of barbecue sausages; Mrs Greenhalgh, our robust but lovable West Country housekeeper, was hanging by her nostrils from a boathook in the hallway, and all the milk-money was missing from the jam-jar by the fridge. it was heart-breaking – £11.45. Three weeks' instalments all gone.

'On top of that, we later discovered that the thieves had taken every one of Suzuki's Aled Jones records – which helped to cheer us up a little bit. But then, when we found that our little dog Patch had been fed Semtex explosive and was now lying in several patches all over the back garden . . . well, that was the point when we decided – enough is enough! Somebody had to put a stop to all this. And that somebody, or rather those somebodies, was . . . were . . . going to be us.'

Julie has a very good point there. Indeed, wasn't it some guy in the Bible who once said, 'The Meek shall inherit the Earth'? Well, whoever he was, he was right. That's us! We're the Meek and we've been downtrodden long enough. Our time has come. The worms are about to turn!

And so now, having ignited the flame of rebellion within their hearts, drawn up a foolproof blueprint for global domination, swilled what's left of Patch down the waste disposal and bought a new dog they've called David Jensen, the Abercorns are ready to help you spearhead the revolution and take over the world – within just one year.

21

But before we can really make a start, there are one or two pressing problems we must deal with, such as finding ourselves somewhere to work from: a secret base of operations tucked aw . . .

Q: *Now, hold it right there, pal!*

Oh, you again.

Q: *It's all very well suggesting that I find myself a base of operations and all that, but what if I only live in a small provincial town on the south coast of England? One which, despite its pleasant aspect and average-to-good facilities, is still out in the bloody sticks? Surely, I'm sunk immediately, aren't I?*

Well, thank you for raising that illuminating point, sir. But, you know, the Abercorns live in a small provincial town called Witchester. It too has a pleasant aspect and average-to-good facilities and is right out in the bloody sticks, but even so, in their new capacity as rebel insurgents and Soldiers of Global Enlightenment, Jeff and Julie couldn't wish for a better place to live.

Let me explain.

Witchester

Witchester is full to bursting with old folks. What was once a tiny, peaceful, out-of-the-way coastal town now seems to suck in thousands of geriatrics each year like a giant suburban Hoover attachment. They have survived two World Wars and, no doubt in some cases, a couple of Ice Ages as well, and now all they do is clog up the best hotels along the seafront, playing canasta and housey-housey for days on end, just waiting for God to pull the plugs on them.

But He doesn't, of course. He's got too much of a sense of humour for that. So in the meantime, and by the miracle of crutch, stick and frame, the Twilighters hobble up and down the promenade each morning in a cloud of camphor, three women to every man, bracing themselves against the piercing easterly gales and wondering if this really is all they've got left to look forward to. Or indeed whether it gets worse.

The town council, for their part, have shunned all trappings of festivity so prevalent in other seaside resorts, opting instead for a rigid 'No-Attractions' policy. That means there are no longer any places of entertainment in the town centre: no cinemas, theatres or pubs. Nor are there any ice-cream vendors on the promenade, selling overpriced cones or drinks-on-sticks from a van – in fact, the only thing you'll find on sticks in Witchester . . . are the inhabitants!

Nothing can disguise the fact that this has become quite the most tedious, bland and annoying place in Britain. So much so, in fact, that the whole town was recently twinned with Paul Daniels.

Hereabouts, they refer to it, rather fondly, as 'Wittie', and thus it was immortalised not long ago in a poem of the same name by local poet, A. Dunlow Sherpod, who lived in the town for over twenty years, before he was jailed for a further twenty for trying to burn the place to the ground.

'Wittie'

Every year, come shine or rain,
Dad put me on the Wittie train,
And packed me off to get my fill,
Of a seaside town where time's stood still.

Where buckets, spades and flags are banned,
And donkeys vetoed off the sand.
No Punch and Judy shows allowed,
Nor anything that draws a crowd.

No theatres, no bars, no flicks,
No crazy golf, no hoops and sticks,
No trams, no buses, no arcades,
No carnivals, no street-parades;
No fights, no crimes, no drunks, no riots . . .
Just OAPs, and peace and quiet.

Now when I hear the Wittie train,
Its noise and clatter once again
Bring back a thousand memories,
Of what a soddin' awful place it is!

A. Dunlow Sherpod

And there you have, in a nutshell, precisely why a small, insignificant town like this will make the ideal cover for the Abercorns' World Domination Plan. So if you live somewhere similar yourself – somewhere depressingly remote, with few, if any, civic amenities, streets lined with invalid carriages and barely a decent shop to speak of, don't knock it. You are starting off with a major advantage.

2

Right, Let's Get Cracking, Then

By far your greatest problem when you set out on a crusade of this magnitude, is finding the money to pay for it.

Taking over the world can be a mighty expensive business, what with submarines and orbital satellites to pay for, plus uniforms, equipment, radar tracking systems, training, research, sweets, missiles, machine guns and other weapons[3] . . . it all adds up. So clearly, what you need first of all is plenty of hard cash – possibly upwards of a hundred million quid, maybe more – and you need it fast!

But how do you get your hands on that kind of money at such short notice, that is the question.

Well, you could always place a swear-box in a television newsroom for a month, that would be one way. Alternatively, what about entering into talks with the billionaire drug barons in Colombia; see if you could sting them for the odd million or two on account? Or you could approach the Mafia, or even Colonel Gadaffi – he always seems to have vast reserves of cash on tap for any dissident or subversive eager to overthrow a Western democracy. Or, if the worst comes to the worst and these methods get you nowhere, then several whist-drives and a string of shrewdly-organised car-boot sales may well be your answer.

If, on the other hand, you want to leave nothing to chance, then there is only one really surefire way to raise a colossal amount of money in such a short space of time, and that is by duping gullible members of the public into giving it to you.

You have two options: either devise a new miracle diet plan

---

[3] For peaceful purposes only, of course.

or start your own religion, it's as simple as that. However, in a book this size, there is really no space to go into these in any great detail.

Q: *What do you mean there's no space? How the hell are we supposed to know what to do if you don't tell us?*

Well, all right, then. But we'll have to squeeze them in before Chapter 3 somehow.

2A

Exploiting the Gullible: Diets

THE DIETING CON-TRICK

Ever since the guy who invented jogging died of heart failure while out jogging, people have been thinking twice before submitting themselves to any of those hard-slog heart-pumping exercise routines. Dieting, by contrast, is still seen as healthy and harmless, and has therefore grown into one of the biggest businesses in the world.

But have you ever wondered why so many new diet-books are produced every year? After all, each one is almost identical to the last, taking an incredible 200 pages or more to state something which is so basic and so obvious to the rest of us that it is barely worth stating at all: i.e. that if you eat less sugar and fat and do more exercise, you'll lose weight.

The reason these books are so successful is that the people who read them are thoroughly weakwilled – after all, that is why they're fat in the first place, isn't it? – and can never stick to a single diet long enough for it to work properly. So when one fails, they try another, then another, forever hopping from book to book, frittering away more and more money, until eventually they throw in the towel, convinced that good health and a decent physique will always be beyond them.

To put it simply, then: if you are prepared to cash in on people's weakness and vanity, the way large parts of the slimming industry do, you'll make an absolute fortune.

The key is to devise a Compleat Health Plan (for some unknown reason, 'complete' is always spelt wrongly when it relates to diets!), consisting of a highly expensive Slimmer

Pack which should, in turn, consist of a sickly powdered milk-shake and stacks of vitamin capsules that the customer has to re-order constantly to maintain his or her supply.

In addition, make sure that any diet you invent includes plenty of carob as its staple ingredient. Nutritionists swear by this stuff and tend to gorge themselves on it like martyrs.

Carob is, in fact, a chocolate-substitute – though not much of one, frankly – which, to the untrained eye, could easily be mistaken for black oil paint. Indeed, most slimmers would sooner eat black oil paint than carob, since it tastes quite vile and when fashioned into the shape of a candy bar, looks like something you might scrape off your shoe after a country walk.

The Compleat Health Diet Plan

In order to market your diet, you should do what the Abercorns have done and set up a new company called Healthruherbs plc., offering a fully-guaranteed weight loss programme to anyone gullible enough to take you up on it.

The Abercorns Compleat Health Diet Plan is made up roughly of the following:

i) *'Lo-Pro': a healthy low protein drink*

Lo-Pro is a sort of milk-shake which Jeff made at home to his own secret formula. It contains herbs, vitamins and minerals – and carob, of course! – plus a splash of cow vaccine and the contents from a few old bottles he found on a shelf at the back of the greenhouse.

The milk-shake in itself will not make you thinner. What it will do is drain all the energy from your body until you can no longer open the fridge door or use a can-opener or even pull the wrapper off a packet of digestive biscuits. That way you are bound to stop putting on weight. Ingenious, eh?

Besides helping you slim, Lo-Pro also contributes towards your overall fitness regime. Repeated vomiting will exercise the stomach and neck muscles, and running backwards and forwards to the lavatory every ten minutes is excellent for strengthening the heart and thighs.

ii) *vitamin supplements*

To be honest, the vitamin tablets make better ear-plugs than they do vitamin tablets. Each one is as big as a child's fist, and almost impossible to swallow unless you ram it down with a rolled-up magazine. Like most tablets, they cost next-to-nothing to produce, contain the bare minimum of active ingredients, and could be an eighth of the size if it weren't for the public's ill-conceived belief that the bigger they are the more good they do you.

iii) *herbal extracts – the biggest con of all*

However, the real secret behind the Healthruherbs Compleat Health Plan lies, as our caption suggests, in the jar of herbal extracts.

Each herbal capsule contains 150mg of pure guarana, a natural amphetamine taken from South American tree-bark, which leaves you feeling as high as a kite, or higher. All dieters are instructed to swallow three of these tablets four times a day every day until they become completely hooked and have to keep re-ordering them time and again to feed their addiction.

The Abercorn Compleat Health Diet Plan costs a stonking £50 every time – imagine, if only a million vain and simple fools are goaded into starting out on the plan, that's £50,000,000 already – half your target total.

For his money, the customer receives all the above, plus a large white promotional badge telling other people that he is a Healthruherbs Diet Victim. The badge says, 'Lose Three Stone, Be Skin and Bone', and must be worn at all times. Even in bed. And finally, there is a book written by Julie, called *Herbal Health Through Healthruherbs*, setting out the diet health plan in full. On the cover is a guarantee that, when you buy it, you will lose ten pounds immediately – which is true, because that's how much the book costs.

Healthruherbs: the success continues.

Prior to marketing the plan nationwide, Jeff has decided to test it out on a willing volunteer, settling in the end for a Mrs Cheesley, who runs a small cafe in Witchester town centre. Aged about 55, Mrs Cheesley is unfit, horribly arthritic and quite obscenely overweight. Indeed, her vital statistics read like the specifications for a gasometer – making her the ideal Healthruherbs customer.

The Healthruherbs Compleat Health Diet Plan in action

Week One. Within days of starting the diet and exactly as planned, Mrs Cheesley becomes hooked on the herbal extract tablets and begins increasing her daily intake in order to feed her steadily worsening addiction. Constant vomiting due to the protein drink means she spends most of her waking hours in front of, or on, or down the lavatory. Overall weight-loss, week one: 11 pounds 10 ounces.

Week Two. Running short of money and regurgitating

more or less round-the-clock by now, Mrs Cheesley begins dealing on the black market in herbal extract tablets, and approaches a few of her friends – Mr and Mrs Patel, the newsasians from the precinct, Mr Peterson, a well-known local hermaphrodite, and Mrs Ford-Clinic, assistant manageress of Witchester's only 24-Hour Reject Wicker Shop. All quickly become hooked on guarana and are soon as high as an elephant's eye. Mrs Cheesley turns over a handsome profit on the deal. Overall weight-loss, week two: 3 stone 4 pounds.

Week Three. Herbal extract tablets are now in short supply. In fact, they're as sparse as an elephant's arse. Mrs Cheesley is arrested for drug offences and charged with being a woman of substances. Copious puking whilst in police custody leads to an early bail application – by the police. Overall weight-loss, week three: 9 stone 2 pounds.

Week Four. Vomiting has finally ceased – principally because her body has turned inside out. Thinner than a rake, Mrs Cheesley toasts the success of the Healthruherbs Compleat Health Plan, together with her GP, a local undertaker and what's left of Mrs and Mrs Patel. Overall weight-loss, final week: 14 stone 10 pounds 7 ounces.

But the soaring success of Healthruherbs needn't stop there. Huge profits can also be made by constantly introducing new products to the range. They don't even have to be health-related, always provided they have great names and good snappy advertising tags.

For example, during the next six months, Jeff plans to expand his catalogue by selling such items as Erectopan Stallion Cream – 'bigger, stronger, firmer, longer'; 'The Vaginal-Whippet' Arousal Stick; Acci-Dent Toothpaste – 'You'll wonder where the sparkle went when you brush your teeth with Acci-Dent'; and Eddovair, a miracle cure for baldness with the tag-line, 'You're never alone with a strand'. Plus a number of bathroom products that trade on international celebrity names, such as Talcum McDowell, Tranquilliser Minnelli, and, at the top of the range, a tube of scrotal jelly that enables older men to have sex three times as often as normal, called Roger More.

31

2B

Exploiting the Gullible: Religion

The Healthruherbs Compleat Health Diet Plan is a brilliant way to rake in a tidy fortune for your cause, but it's by no means the best way. For, when it comes to raising gigantic amounts of cash in the shortest period of time, nothing, I say *nothing*, can compare with the revenue you will generate by starting your own religion.

There are several books available which tell you exactly how to go about becoming a major spiritual leader. One in particular, *You Too Can Be Pope!* by Mitsi Eekhof-Stork, lays down the crucial factors necessary to founding a successful – and by that, of course, I mean lucrative – religious sect.

Summed up briefly, these are your six steps to Heaven:

Step One: Which religion do I choose?
Any one you like, pal, it hardly matters; they're all in roughly the same state of decay. Though if you take my advice you will start a brand new religion all of your own.

Jeff, for instance, has noted the total disenchantment which ordinary people feel towards established religion these days, and the way they are turning away from it in their millions. They may have a point, too. I mean, you only have to tot up the number of earthquakes and famines that have happened recently, not to mention all the train crashes, motorway pile-ups and air disasters, to come to the inevitable conclusion that either God has taken to behaving in distinctly more mysterious ways than usual, or else He doesn't exist at all and we've simply been fooling ourselves all along.

If this is how *you* feel, then you are not alone.

Jeff suspects that he has come along at the right time and spotted a gap in the market. After all, there are dozens of religions catering for people who believe in God. Surely it's about time there was one for those who don't. It could be called **Faitheism**, where membership is not based on belief in a set of fundamental spiritual principles. All that matters is: have you got lots of money in the bank and are you prepared to hand it over to the Church when told to do so?

It will take a little time to sort things out, but the Abercorns are planning to open up their garage as a makeshift chapel, calling it the Most Unholy Church of St Thomas the Doubter, with Jeff as both Archbishop and head preacher – a sort of Billy Graham, only without the laughs.

Step Two: Decide what your message to your followers is
   going to be

Any old crap will do, frankly; the more unfathomable the better – particularly if you haven't a clue what you're talking about.

I suggest you preach a mixture of love and forgiveness for starters, then maybe spin them the old yarn about everlasting life, and finish up with a promise that they will all surely go to Heaven – *but only* if they empty the entire contents of their bank accounts into yours within the next twenty-four hours. This is the 'Pray As You Earn' system and thousands of bogus Messiahs right down through the ages have got very rich by using it.

'But surely, they'll suss me out,' you're saying. 'I'll never get away with that.'

Why not? Hundreds of churches already do. It's just one of those old quirks of human nature, I guess, that people seem to enjoy handing their hard-earned savings over to fanatics and nutcases they've never even met.

In North America particularly, God's love is seen as a tradable commodity, something that can be bought and sold in bulk, like margarine or videos, simply by giving some loud-mouthed evangelist the number of your credit-card, and then praying a lot. Many churches these days do what Robin Hood never could: they rob from the poor to keep for themselves, and offer you a unique unmissable opportunity to pay off your conscience in the process. The result? You feel fifty times better for having given the money, the Church feels fifty times wealthier for having taken it, and God doesn't care either way. He just wants you to be rich, successful and happy. How you get there is your own business.

One last thing: I know that all you want is the money, but if you are going to make a halfway-convincing Messiah, I'm afraid you will also need to know your stuff, and by that I mean the Scriptures. To doubt something, you have at least to understand it in the first place. You can't simply 'muddle through' by watching old reruns of *Moses the Lawgiver* and reciting the lyrics to *Jesus Christ Superstar*, hoping they won't notice, because they will!

Step Three: Spreading the Word

Your best bet, to begin with anyway, is to deliver your message about Faitheism in the way other religions do – by distributing shoddy photostatted leaflets in the street and around your neighbourhood door to door.

Each leaflet should be no bigger than a Ford Granada – in fact, considerably smaller if possible: pocket-size will do, with a simple line-drawing on the front, showing Jeff posing in some kind of Biblical setting, surrounded by bluebirds and sheep and children of different colours (*who are not carrying skateboards!*) – together with some well-known quote from the Scriptures underneath to make it sound sort of official – a brief passage from St Paul's Letters to the Philistines will get you by. Or, if you're not absolutely *au fait* with the Gospels, then a couple of lines from *HMS Pinafore* should suffice. They'll never know the difference.

Above all, make sure your religion has a sexy image. Don't give the leaflet a boring name, such as 'The War Cry' (Salvation Army) or 'The Watchtower' (Jehovah's Witnesses). Instead, make it saucy. Call it 'Cavort' or 'Licky-Licky' or 'Wet Dreams,' something tantalising and erotic. And try to ensure that you exclude all references to God, Heaven, everlasting life and the rest. Stick to what sells.

Before you know it, you'll be streets ahead of your rivals.

Very soon it'll be 'So long, Sally Army', 'Goodbye, God Squad', 'See you, C.U.'. It's amazing what you can do with a little persistence, some ruthless skulduggery and a few photos of randy firm-breasted Spanish waitresses dog-paddling in a tank of Brylcreem.

If in doubt, remember this equation: more sales+more converts=MORE MONEY!!

Step Four: Make your religion heaps of fun
This should be the reigning principle of your crusade.

Your religious service must be enjoyable, otherwise nobody will turn up. Many old-time religions use popular music to pull in the crowds – the Rhythm Methodists, for instance – so always try to mix the meat-and-two-veg of standard spiritual teachings with a side-salad of shouting, dancing and communal singing. Chants would be a fine thing, so maybe you could include some of those as well.

The formula for the celebration is simple: plenty of forgiveness, love, sharing, caring, gratitude, and so on. Most ordinary people are crying out for someone, *anyone*, to show interest in them and their problems, so all you have to do is display even the teensiest speck of concern for them and they'll be swarming around your church like lepidopterists around a moth.

On top of all this, make sure you organise guest appearances by local country and western artists, such as Rich Pickens. Get him to sing his sixties' classic, 'Jesus was the Getaway Driver in God's Dawn-Raid on My Soul' plus a medley of other hits he's had banned from Radio 2. If for some reason he can't make it, you could try that toe-tapping country-dance trio, The Four Morrismen of the Apocalypse. Or even Twisted Sister if you can get them. Just make it fun, that's all. Don't turn your service into a pantomime, that would be unkind, but do try to bring in performers who have some gospel-singing experience as well as a repertoire of modern-day hits.

Where do you find the names of these religious performers? Try the Book of Acts!

Step Five: What kind of followers do you wish to attract? Of course, it's almost impossible to generalise – everyone everywhere in the whole world would agree with me on that! – but as a rule, you should try and target *the disenfranchised minorities* within society.

There are millions of them all over the country: poor and needy folks who feel they have been abandoned by the rest of us. Go out and appeal to them, offer them the hand of friendship, win them over to your side. Then, not only will you have a pool of people always on hand to help you in your crusade, but also when the time comes for you to seize political power as well, you'll have millions of electors ready and waiting to vote for you. You'll clean up at the polls.

The government won't complain or prevent you from taking them in. After all, you're performing a valuable public service, a sort of human refuse-collection, unburdening society of its unwanted dregs and removing thousands of paupers and hangers-on from the social services register.

Q: *But what the hell will I do if thousands of these grubby horrible people insist on joining my Church? Where will I put them all?*

Do what the Abercorns have done. They plan to turn 17, Campbell Avenue into an open commune, a sunny welcoming place for anyone prepared to make Witchester their spiritual heartland. When this happens, the value of neighbouring properties in the street will plummet, the owners will be desperate to move out and Jeff can snap up their houses at knock-down prices, ready to accommodate even more converts.

Q: *All right, so what kind of people are we talking about here?*

I can't be too specific, as you might expect, but you might like to invite some of the following to join your following:
childless one-parent families (male) and childless one-parent families (female), followed by all sycophants, hypocrites, outcasts, outlaws, prostitutes, gays, lesbians, muggers, druggies, gypsies, tramps and thieves. Also

expected are the weak, the weary, the clueless, the kooky and the strange; the diseased, the depressed, the discouraged, the downtrodden, the forgotten and neglected. And finally, all of society's bores, including assistant bank managers, chartered accountants, electricity board meter readers, court officials and shorthand writers; librarians of more than thirty-five years standing; judges of more than thirty-five years sitting; addicts of defunct science fiction TV series – Trekkies, Whovians, members of 'Fanderson', the 'Six of One Society' and the rest; train-spotters, traction engine rally organisers; double-glazing salesmen; anyone who collects elastic; whingeing old women on radio phone-ins ('I never miss your programme, Derek. I'm 79 and an invalid . . .'); those dowdy, clueless chaps with painstakingly-arranged scoop-over hairstyles who work behind the enquiry desk in tax offices; and, lastly, anyone holding himself out to be an expert ('I'm not saying that butterscotch *does* cause brain tumours, but our tests show . . .' etc).

'We want *YOU*' says Jeff. 'All of you. Become a Faitheist and see the world. In fact, take over the world! It's yours for the asking.'

Oh yes, and one final tip before I forget.

Step Six: Get the Queen involved somehow

Once your religion is off and running, try to persuade the Queen to be head of it. She almost certainly won't want to be, of course – this is one busy lady we're talking about here. And after all, she's got a Church of her own to run. But, nevertheless, keep writing. Having Her Majesty on your letterhead somehow legitimises the whole affair and lends no end of credibility to your cause, especially when you're out begging for money.

Her role needn't be a large one: handing out hymnbooks at the service would be a nice touch, or picking up litter, or even ringing the bells for an hour beforehand: nothing too demanding. Whatever happens, though, don't be afraid to ask – she might say yes! It would certainly make a change from sitting in the back of a car for hours waving at total strangers, or planting saplings on blustery November days in Cheshire and having to visit Tasmania year-in year-out.

Mind you, if she does start making feeble excuses and trying to dodge her responsibilities, then simply threaten her with abolition. When the revolution comes, we won't be needing a royal family anyway, and so she and her kind will be out on their bloody ear straight away, corgis and all! A threat like this should inflame her worry-glands considerably, after which it's a safe bet that Her Maj. will fall in with any scheme you care to propose.

However, if you feel that the Queen's excuse is a genuine one, you could always try Princess Michael of Kent instead (or Rent-A-Kent, as she's affectionately known in some quarters), or even, if you're really strapped, the Duchess of Argyll. Basically, any royal, however minor, can rake in millions for your cause, so don't give up.

Q: *Excuse me.*

Yes?

Q: *Surely, if I decide to start a religion, I've got to have real rules and principles. I can't keep quoting from* HMS Pinafore *indefinitely, or else my followers might begin to suspect something.*

Ah, right. True.

Q: *So . . . ?*

So yes, you must have a set of well-knitted principles that, on cursory inspection, make some kind of sense. To help you, Jeff has compiled a brief, easy-to-follow, cut-out-and-keep guide explaining how religions work and also setting out fairly comprehensively the principles that anyone who claims to be a Faitheist should believe in.

So without further ado, let's saddle up the donkey of religious theory, and take a short ride along the sands of Controversy Beach, as Mrs Greenhalgh might say – though it's not very likely.

Jeff says . . .

I. *So what's this Faitheism lark all about, Jeff?*

Well, I'm determined not to get bogged down with anything so tedious as accuracy at this stage, so let's skip quickly over the facts and get right down to the juicy bits.

Basically, Faitheists all share a deep, longstanding and incontrovertible belief that God probably doesn't exist.

Other religions don't agree, of course. They regard 'God' as being some . . . well . . . Being, I suppose. A big . . . *thing* – sitting out there in the darkness, like an isolated viewer in an empty movie theatre, scrutinising us, judging us, deciding our fate with a flick of His hand; indiscriminately killing some, rescuing others, answering a few prayers, turning down a few more. Well, take it from me, this just ain't so. (If you're currently a regular churchgoer, then I'm sorry to have to be the first to break the bad news to you. It's rather like being told that there's no such thing as Santa Claus. Although, come to think of it, it's quite possible that you didn't know *that* either, in which case these last couple of pages will have been a bit of a downer all round, I should imagine.)

The Good News, though, is that there *is* something out there – a force, an energy, call it what you will – which unites, regulates and permeates each one of us, and which causes the trees to grow, the seasons to change, and so on. But because it is only a force, it's neutral. You can't bargain with it, plead for its mercy, fight on its behalf, be judged by it, or anything else that you might do if you were talking about a solid Being, a Divine Figure, a God.

Try looking on it as the Celestial Electricity Supply. By trusting it and believing in it, you're just plugging your mind and body into the mains – 'The Celestial Grid'.

What I'm really saying, I guess, is that you shouldn't allow other people's interpretation of the way the universe works, however potent or persuasive it may be, to influence your behaviour. They don't understand it any more than you do.

II. *Hmmm, strong stuff. But religion is important to millions of people. You can't just write it off.*

Sure. But organised religion is just a set of rules and regulations like any other, save that, even if you abide by them strictly, they by no means guarantee you a greater measure of happiness or contentment than someone who disobeys them.

However, religion is a very clever device. Indoctrinating huge numbers of people is a highly complex process involving mass hypnosis on a colossal scale. It involves the use of three factors which must be present in any religious service:

i) *A point of fixation:* normally, it's a cross, but in your case, anything will do: a statue, a flag, an emblem, even a photograph of yourself – whatever you like, provided the crowd has something before them which they can focus on and which embodies in a single powerful symbol all the teachings and beliefs of the organisation to which it relates.

ii) *A raised platform or pulpit:* vital for any kind of mass hypnosis. Whenever you tip your head back and look up towards a raised object, it causes a blast of alpha waves in the brain and a trance-inducing chemical called serotonin is released into your bloodstream. That is why the pulpit in a church was originally a raised platform – to get people to look up for long periods during the service so that they could be hypnotised quicker.

iii) *Mass chanting:* anything from hymns to prayers will do, just so long as it affords an opportunity to your followers to repeat in unison messages that endorse the common cause. It also helps induce hypnosis if the congregation is made to stand up and sit down at regular intervals, as this disorientates them and makes them more vulnerable to trance.

III. *But all of this doesn't account for the idea of Hell, for instance. Surely, that does exist.*

Faitheists don't believe so. To us, Hell is a hoax.

The Church has always been an arm of government, don't forget that; and religion is a traditional method for keeping people in their place within society. 'Conform or don't,' is the threat. 'It's up to you. But if you don't believe in what we believe in, you'll go to Hell and be damned for all time.' And, quite naturally, you don't want to go to Hell, do you? Nobody does. It sounds a horrible place – even though you'll be dead when you get there. But don't be taken in. Tell them what Jeff says: Hell is just a clever fiction dreamed up by churchmen over the centuries as a desperate measure to make ordinary people like us toe the line and hand over huge sums of money to the State.

IV. *And Heaven . . . ?*

Same. Sorry.

V. *Bloody hell! So what should I do now, then?*

Simple. Join the Most Unholy Church of St Thomas the Doubter without delay. Become a Faitheist, a true religious non-believer, a Soldier of Enlightenment, and change the world. There are millions of frightened, baffled souls out there just waiting to hear our message. Deliver it lovingly, practise it diligently, and reap its rewards lucratively.

That's it. Back to the book!

3

The Badger's Rectum

Now that you have worked out how to make huge sums of money to support this World Domination campaign of yours, it's time you thought about setting up a terrorist organisation as well. Make this an early priority.

Q: Hang on! **What** *terrorist organisation?? I thought this was supposed to be a peaceful movement.*

It is. But you must understand that ruling the whole planet is not a straightforward task. It is unpredictable and dangerous and will require ingenuity, daring and courage if you are to emerge victorious in twelve months' time, bearing the title of President of the World. So you have to ensure that, whilst you are out there presenting to the public the smiling, convivial, sympathetic face of your revolutionary cause, someone else is lurking in the shadows and getting on with the real dirty work.

Behind every saint there is a sinner, or so they say, and you should try to recruit several dozen sinners very early on to help you in your mission: a crack team of soldiers, forever on standby, ready to protect your interests at home and abroad.

SETTING UP A TERRORIST CELL
The most important rule is to give your organisation a good name. In fact, it is so important that I am going to say it again, only this time in bold type.
   Give your organisation a good name.
   There.
   At first sight, choosing a name may seem a frivolous task, particularly when there are so many other pressing matters to

attend to. But, on the contrary, any movement aiming to make its mark on society must seek huge amounts of publicity for itself through the newspapers and TV. But before the media can give you any coverage at all, they must know what to call you. A sad rule of life, I'm afraid, but a strict one.

Everything has to be called something; even things which, on the face of it, could get by without having a name: comets, for instance, or locomotives, or giraffes in zoos, or cross-Channel ferries, hurricanes and space shuttles, will nevertheless be given one, usually by the press, so that whatever-it-is may then be slotted into its own special stereotype group, where it can be pigeon-holed alongside all the other whatever-they-ares and filed away for future reference.

In fact, if you don't call something *something*, then the pressmen will go behind your back and do it for you. That is why your average pet mouse in a news story tends to be nicknamed Mickey; a rabbit will be called Roger or Bugs, a bear Winnie, and a donkey Hôté. All terribly predictable. Similarly, parrots are seldom anything but Polly, ducks are Donald (after the legendary cartoon character), and elephants Gerald (after the legendary jazz and blues singer).

So what sort of name should you go for?

Well, my advice is: choose something that will sound good when it's reported on news bulletins, but which also reflects your purpose as rebel insurgents, renegades, dangermen and outlaws.

Something moderately idealistic will do, something that spits at you and suggests that, although you believe in peace and goodwill and understanding between all races and creeds, you wouldn't hesitate to shoot the knackers off any bastard who so much as nicked your parking space – understood? I mean, we're meek but we're not cissies, right?

Also, try and make it catchy, like an advertising jingle. Choose a name which lingers in the memory long after you've heard it, and which could be pronounced by even the most half-witted journalists (roughly two-thirds of them!). Above all, avoid any combination of those three vastly overworked words: People, Liberation and Front. That means *no* 'Liberated Front of the People', *no* 'People's Revolutionary

Liberation Front', and *definitely no* 'People's Revolutionary Front for the Liberation of other People's Revolutionary Fronts'.

Why not?

Well, there are just too many similar groups around already, all claiming to be pro-liberation-this and pro-revolutionary-that. They're all very much of a muchness, usually fighting endlessly over a mere matter of principle or laying down their lives to save some odd bit of land that is barren and quite worthless and which nobody in his right mind would want anyway.

So be original at all costs, that's my advice, and if you still can't decide what to call yourselves, then do what the Abercorns did: take a poll. Invite written suggestions from each member of your household and see what turns up. The resulting list might look something like this:

a) *Guerrillas in the Mist* (ridiculous)
b) *The Pals of Palestine* (Revolutionary People's Liberation Front) (too corny, and what did I just say about using crap names like this?)
c) *The Friends of Beatrix Potter* (ideal if you plan to terrorise wooded glades and riverbanks, otherwise it's too fluffy by half and unlikely to be taken seriously on the world political stage)
d) *Terror Firma* (catchy, anarchic – a possible) and
e) *The Vicious Circle* (smacks slightly of devil-worship. Even so, it's not bad. Another possible).

When a vote was taken by Jeff, 85% opted for Terror Firma as being by far the most sensible, sinister and memorable name for the non-violent political wing of a religious organisation Hell-bent, or rather Heaven-bent, on global power. A tiny minority, just 10%, consisting of Julie and Mrs Greenhalgh, chose The Friends of Beatrix Potter; whilst a piddling 5%, in other words Suzuki, voted for The Pals of Palestine (Revolutionary People's Liberation Front), for which she was given a good spanking and locked in her room for nine days without solids.

Recruiting volunteers

You will have to decide quite early on what sort of people you want as members of Terror Firma.

Of course, even the tiniest amount of intelligence would be an asset, and therefore each candidate should be made to sit a small IQ test right at the start – nothing too taxing, just a few fairly general questions to help sort out the intellectual wheat from the neanderthal chaff. Something along the lines of:

a) 'If it takes 25 seconds for one man to piss in a public lavatory when he's alone . . . how long will it take if two other men are watching him over the top of the urinal?'

b) 'Tutte Lemkow played the part of Schmoltz in *which* classic fifties Ealing comedy?'

c) 'Anita Harris is an entertainer.' Discuss.

d) 'Peter buys a family-sized bag of Revels. He puts seven in one pocket, five in another and gives the rest to Birgut, an enigmatic Belgian dental receptionist he met on a recent canal-boating holiday in Leicestershire. But there is a hole in his trousers and he loses three Revels immediately. Of those that are left he eats the first, finds it is one of those horrible sticky coconutty things, regurgitates it and puts it back in the bag, hands four to his mother for safekeeping, gives five to Michael Jackson's sister Latoya, and puts the remainder in a small tin on the dining room table. Much to his surprise, next day, he finds twenty more half-eaten Revels under the cooker. So he divides these equally between his twin brothers, Ted and Jennifer, and Latoya Jackson, who is still hanging around outside the house for some reason! Of the remaining eight chocolates, he eats four more, loses two down the back of the sofa, gives Birgut one and flushes the remaining five away. Then he catches the next train to Folkestone, takes a huge cocaine overdose and throws himself off a cliff. Why?'

As their new recruits flock through the front door, the Abercorns greet them warmly with a jeroboam of 7-Up, a glass of Jeff's home-made Crimplene wine, a red-hot slice of Mrs Greenhalgh's delicious dangleberry pie, plus a specially-prepared bowl of prawn dildos with a sweet-n-sour dip.

For her part, Julie has written 'The Meek shall inherit the

Earth, if that's all right with you . . . Please say if it isn't . . .' in Magic Marker on an old bedsheet, and strung it up across the front of the house, and Suzuki is playing 'Stairway to Heaven' on her Stylophone.

Everyone agrees, it's a fabulous day all round and, in Jeff's opinion, the start of something really quite important.

Of course, the Abercorns have no say in how your own non-violent terrorist wing is to be constituted; that lies solely within your discretion. However, Jeff has decided that, of those who passed the IQ test, he will be recruiting only committed longterm lesbians to fight in his crack insurgence units. Twenty lesbians should be quite enough to meet his immediate needs.

'But why lesbians, Jeff?' you're asking. 'Surely they're moral reprobates, disowned by God and shunned by all upstanding, right-thinking members of society.'

Jeff says . . .

'Hmmmm, well put! But here's why.'

a) *Butchness*. Lesbians revel shamelessly in their sexuality and won't hesitate to prove that they're as good as, if not better than, the next man. They would think nothing, for

46

example, of spending an entire morning lugging heavy printing equipment up a steep slope at shoulder height, or shifting three dozen Steinway pianos down eight flights of stairs and then carrying them to the North of Scotland on their backs.

These days, firms of lesbian builders are springing up all over the country, with the motto, 'Let a Les Build Your Res'. So by using female homosexuals, you're merely swimming with the popular tide and won't offend anyone – except maybe female homosexuals.

b) *Motivation*. Many are ex-CND members, and practically all of them are out-and-out socialists too.

After years spent handcuffing each other to missiles on news bulletins, the recent diffusion of East/West tensions has, to be honest, come as quite a blow to them. They view the current trend towards multilateral disarmament with a tremendous sadness and sense of betrayal. However, times move on, and they have had to make themselves busy elsewhere. A few have recently resurfaced to protect the rights of unborn babies, branding themselves 'pro-life', and picketing abortion clinics with the cry, 'You can beat us and mistreat us, but you'll never defoetus.' The rest, though, are waiting for another cause to come along which fires them sufficiently to be worth fighting for.

Without doubt, world domination is that cause!

c) *Health*. Lesbians rarely, if ever, suffer from sexually-transmitted diseases – which is just as well, especially in this day and AIDS.

d) *Ease of identification*. All lesbians have tough, knock-about names. Nine out of ten will be called either Roz, Les, Steph, Trish or Bev.

e) *Economics*. They tend to dress mostly in clothes that are plain, unfeminine and which, above all, make them wholly unenticing to men.

Anyone wishing to convert to a lifestyle of lesbianism should therefore take care to observe the following strict dress-code: standard-issue chocolate-brown V-neck tank-top, available from British Home Stores or selected branches of Milletts, with a lumberjack shirt underneath, chocolate brown slacks, and a pair of flat functional shoes – preferably with leather uppers and woman-made soles.

Since they come with a uniform already provided, this makes them extremely cost-effective as a fighting force.

f) *Unpleasant*. They also have no sense of humour to speak of, and so won't fritter away precious hours engaging in needless horseplay like men do. In fact, to the average male, lesbian humour is well-nigh unfathomable; e.g. popular lesbian joke:

> 'My dog's got no nose.'
> 'How does he smell?'
> 'I just told you – he's got no nose!'

See? Baffling.

Q: *But hang on a minute. Neither my wife nor I is a lesbian, and I wouldn't say we go a whole bundle on homosexuality generally, but surely, you're being totally, deplorably homophobic here. It's disgraceful. Someone ought to set the law on you, pal! This is a scandal.*

Thank you for raising that particularly astute point, Sir. Would you mind, though, if I returned to the matter a little later?

Q: *Well . . . I dunno . . .*

Please . . . ?

Q: *Oh, all right, then, but just make sure you do!*

It's a promise.

Thanks, Jeff!

Finding a front for your Front

There must be a number of places you could choose as a suitable secret base for your organisation, but by far the best choice would be a local cafe or tea-bar, since, with that kind of cover, nobody would ever notice the regular comings and goings of masked gunmen, religious fanatics, insurgence teams and world leaders, as they pop in and out of the building for top-level talks and the odd nocturnal rendezvous.

By sheer luck, it just so happens that Julie is good friends with Mrs Cheesley who, together with her husband, affectionately known by one and all as 'Mr Cheesley', runs a little tea-room off the High Street called the 'Cafe Come Home'. They're a sweet couple – he is a retired dentist, she is the wife of a retired dentist – although alas, these days, both of them are awfully arthritic and mostly bedbound, thanks to years spent jogging and attending keep-fit classes. And in addition, Mrs Cheesley is now suffering from anorexia, blindness and creeping paralysis after her recent run-in with the Health-ruherbs Compleat Health Diet Plan.

All of which means that they find the day-to-day upkeep of their restaurant business an impossible burden to bear.

At first, however, they were rather reluctant to allow their little cafe to be used as a front for terrorist activities, at least not without some kind of compensation. But, following a good deal of coherent explanation about the project by Jeff and Julie, and also some additional persuasion from Mrs Greenhalgh and her lucky rolling pin, they began to see many considerable pluses to the idea of world domination after all, and finally consented to their tea-room being used as a cover for the organisation.

Disguising Your Hideaway

Unfortunately, the downside of the secret cafe hideaway idea is that, unless you are very careful indeed, it may at some point start to attract customers: complete strangers who drop in for coffee and a Danish just as you're about to eavesdrop on NATO defence transmissions, or unravel maps of British ground-to-air missile installations and show them to a few friends.

So what can you do to keep customers away?

Well, the Abercorns have decided to tackle the problem in three ways, and you would do well to follow suit:

1) First, change the name of the business from 'Cafe Come Home', which sounds too cosy and pleasant by half, to something a touch less welcoming, such as The 'Bugger Off, We're Closed' Bar and Grill, for instance, or, better still, 'The Badger's Rectum'. A name like this is dignified, to-the-point and plausible, I'm sure you'd agree, yet at the

same time guaranteed to be wholly offputting to passing trade.

2) Be sure to price yourself right out of the market. £25.50 for a glass of milk should keep all but the most lactatious customer away. In addition, you could charge £38.00 for a pot of tea for two, with toasted sandwiches beginning at a foolhardy £155 for a basic cheese and tomato, and going up to £357.50 if the customer insists on the filling actually being inside the sandwich when he gets it.

Also, when drawing up the bill, be as awkward as you can. No major credit cards to be accepted, of course, or even minor ones, come to that. And stipulate clearly that the only cheques that will be taken are those drawn on the First National Bank of Tobago – *if*, and only if, they are accompanied by a letter of reference from the manager, and then only if each cheque has been countersigned individually by Aretha Franklin.

3) Lastly, wherever possible, make the food quite ghastly, and be sure to advertise the fact clearly in your window. Be as graphic as you can and try including a few home-made delicacies. For instance: the lining from a grey squirrel's bottom (when in season); tortoise-heads in a rich white gravy, which may or may not taste of turpentine, depending on how much you put in; Pot Noodle.

Mmmmm, scrummy yummy!

Once you have recruited your lesbian units and given them a secret undercover base to work from, they should be poised for action at a moment's notice; there must be none of this sitting-around-smoking-and-playing-gin-rummy-for-days-on-end nonsense, the way Nicaraguan Freedom Fighters appear to. In fact, the only time guerrillas and mercenaries ever really seem to do anything constructive towards their cause, it strikes me, is when a foreign TV newscrew turns up to film them – at which point, they rush out of their tents in a mad panic and start blitzing the war zone with missiles and mortars, so that sympathetic governments abroad will witness the appalling pain and suffering being inflicted upon innocent lives and will send them huge amounts of money in overseas aid to buy more weapons with.

Well, this kind of behaviour may earn you a string of medals in South America, my friend, but it's not the way we do things here.

If you honestly believe that World Domination is a cause worth fighting for, then you should ensure that your ground-troops are fit for action around-the-clock, and that means they must be properly trained and equipped – a highly expensive operation requiring dozens of extra personnel. In fact, taking over the world will be a full-time occupation for several hundred people, some doing research and drawing up plans and blueprints, that sort of thing, while others are busy faking passports with a set of multi-coloured Biros, supplying made-up information to embassies to obtain false visas, packing nutritious lunches for the Soldiers of Enlightenment and generally beavering away day and night to get everything tied up in time. Needless to say, this is personnel the Abercorns simply don't have as yet. Or rather, they *didn't* have until recently – until Julie came up with a quick and easy solution: pensioners.

Brilliant!

Witchester is teeming with old folk, all of them either slumped comatose in deck-chairs along the sea-front, or else huddled together in bus-shelters out of the wind, waiting to be given something useful to do with what is left of their empty lives. Many of our smaller towns are top-heavy with pen-sioners just like Witchester, so why don't you be the person to help them out? Let them know they still have a purpose in life. For, as Julie reminds us . . .

'You must never dismiss the elderly, the wheelchair-bound, the sick and the dying, they all have their part to play in the Revolution.

'Society would like to be rid of them, of course. Governments see them as a burden and a major drain on the social services, but to us, they are something else entirely: friends, helpers, advisers, cheap labour . . . they're like gold-dust. So try and make them feel wanted; help give them back their self-esteem by letting them do something useful towards the Revolution. Sentry duty, for example: guarding your HQ against infiltration by rebel insurgents . . .'

Sentry duty.

'Rigorous stuff! Just what they like!

'And always be sure to keep your geriatric support teams fit and happy by making plenty of provision for entertainments in their off-duty hours: organise singalongs, bingo sessions, Terence Trent d'Arby lookalike contests; better still, let them play the odd game of "Senior Just-A-Minute", in which contestants have to talk for exactly sixty seconds on a given subject without hesitation, repetition, or droning on and on about the War and how much better everything was in the Good Old Days.

'This is the least we can do for our old folks. After all, we owe them such a lot.'

That is typical of Julie. So caring, so giving.

Firearms training

Not strictly necessary, I suppose, since ours is to be a peaceful backdoor revolution, conducted, wherever possible, without pain or bloodshed. But even so, your lesbian troops should be taught to handle firearms properly just in case things turn nasty along the way.

To have a gun you must also have a licence, and I'm sure I needn't remind you that any weapon in your possession, whether it's a powerful Baryshnikov rifle, or a Torville & Dean 5.8mm revolver, or even one of those shotguns used specifically for firing at nuns, a Carmelite rifle, it should be kept for peaceful purposes only . . .

However, that doesn't mean you can't defend yourself when under attack, simply that you should resort to alternative methods wherever possible.

Q: *Yes, but what do you mean by 'alternative'? If not guns, what are we going to use?*

Since you ask, our chief weapon is to be the potato peeler . . .

Q: *Of course it is. I can't think why I didn't guess that myself. The potato peeler . . . tsk, it's so obvious really, isn't it?*

Never underestimate the potato peeler,[4] a utensil with so many varied and fascinating uses it is practically impossible to list them all here – although most of them, I admit, are not unconnected with peeling potatoes. What a lot of people don't realise, however, is just how versatile the ordinary household peeler can be. For example, in an emergency, it can double as an extremely effective missile when fired from a standard coastguard's flare gun . . .

. . . and is easily adaptable for use in a variety of other combat situations, too.

Camouflage

Again, there is no space in a book of this size to go into great detail, but suffice it to say that your lesbian units should be taught at least the basics of camouflage and shown a few simple ways to blend in with their surroundings in the event of enemy attack.

---

[4] I refer, of course, to hand-held peelers only and not to the Kenwood Chef potato-peeling attachment which makes a cumbersome weapon in any battle and is also a bugger to carry over long distances. *Historical note:* Extensive operational tests carried out during the Falklands Campaign show that had a Kenwood Chef been used, then Port Stanley might never have been recaptured at all, simply because the flex wouldn't have been long enough.

For instance, Jeff is now fully camouflaged. Can you spot him in this picture?

What to do with your lesbians next

Right, well, having recruited, equipped and trained them, the next thing to do is split them into two equal teams.

It doesn't matter how they divide up – you could try 'Tallest versus Smallest', or 'Vegetarians versus Carnivores', or 'Those who hate olives versus those who can't stand marzipan', or even 'People who think "No More Lonely Nights" is Paul McCartney's greatest song', versus 'C. Moonites, Yesterdayists and Mull-of-Kintyrophiles' – any way you like, just so long as you end up with two groups of ten.

These are your Crack Lesbian Insurgence Teams, elite groundtroops, on call day and night to tackle any mission, any task, however dangerous or far-fetched; willing to sacrifice themselves in the cause of World Domination and prepared to do anything at all to help you win the fight – except perhaps kissing a fella, which would be just too horrible to contemplate.

Jeff's guerrilla units are made up of Mrs Greenhalgh's daughter Lucette and a few of her friends, plus one or two others they picked up in a notorious gay pub near Witchester, called The Old Bulge and Bush.

Once trained, each team is then allotted a specific task.

C.L.I.T. 1 – assignment

To the first team – consisting of Rozes 1 and 4, three of the Stephs, the odd Trish or two, and Bevs 8 to 10 – falls the heavyweight job of digging a tunnel between the Abercorns' nuclear bunker 'Sea View', and their HQ at The Badger's Rectum, so that, in the event of a siege or a raid by the SAS (or indeed by *any* Scandinavian Airline, come to that), or even Flying Squad detectives, then the whole family will have a sure-fire escape route.

C.L.I.T. 2 – assignment

Meantime, to Group Two – made up mostly of Bevs, but with a couple of Stephs and the final Roz as well, and commanded by Lesbo-in-Chief Lucette – is given the rather more difficult mission of infiltrating the media, a campaign which they have codenamed, because everything has to be called something, Operation Redgrave.

OPERATION REDGRAVE:
Infiltrating the Media

Try to look at this as part of your overall longterm strategy, in which you aim to win widespread political support amongst the general public – enough support, in fact, to help you unseat the present government and take control of the country.

Now, at first glance, overthrowing a democracy like ours may seem to be an impossible task – but not so. There are a number of ways you could go about it. For instance, you could do it the hard way, by winning the hearts and minds of the electorate and persuading them that your revolutionary aims are realistic and worthwhile, and then engaging in an extended campaign of reasoned argument and debate over many months leading up to an election, the way real politicians do. A very fair way of doing things, to be sure: highly democratic and honest. Although, on the minus side, it is also extremely bureaucratic and longwinded. Just think of all the form-filling, campaigning, protocol and propaganda you would have to endure, not to mention the endless committee-meetings you must attend, speeches you will need to make, etc etc. And even then the bastards will probably go behind your back and vote for someone else. Democracy sucks, doesn't it, eh?

Anyway, speed is of the essence here. Working your way up through conventional channels like this would take far too long. What is needed instead is something a little spicier: a fast-acting, foolproof programme of sabotage and subversion which, if started straight away, would produce big results by the end of the book.

Somehow you must steer the electorate around to your way of thinking, so that they vote for you in their millions long before they ever realise what is happening. And the only way to do that is to brainwash them!

Practical Exercise: Kidnapping a Tycoon

Codename: Project Vanessa

I'll come straight to the point: you have to find a senior figure within the communications industry, the biggest cheese you can lay your hands on, and kidnap him. Simple as that!

You won't have to look far for one. We're probably talking about five or six possible people in the whole world – businessmen whose corporate interests transcend international boundaries, taking in newspapers, radio, TV and satellite stations, record companies, publishing, the lot, in dozens of countries right across the globe.

These are what we refer to as The Men In Blue Suits. Together with other top professionals in banking, politics, retailing, finance, oil exporting, arms trading and drug-trafficking, they rule the world as it stands today, with just a little help from the Church, the CIA, MI5, KGB, UHT (the French Secret Service) and sundry underworld factions dotted around here and there. However, by far the most influential and powerful of all these are the men who own and control the media.

The influence which media-moguls exert over the way ordinary people live their lives, through what they read or what they see on television, is almost incalculable. It therefore makes perfect sense for you to abduct one of these big-shot tycoons as soon as possible and win him over to your way of thinking. With the Big Cheese on your side, you will have a direct channel to the thoughts and behaviour-patterns of a gigantic cross-section of the global population.

Q: *Excuse me.*

Yes – what now?

Q: *I'd like a private word with you please. Would you care to join me in the footnotes for a moment?*

'Oh, very well . . .'[1]

Righto. Well, anyway, luckily for us, the Abercorns have decided not to kidnap anyone after all . . .

Q: *Thank you.*

Don't mention it . . . Instead, they have opted for an altogether more subtle technique, and the victim they have chosen is none other than multi-millionaire newspaper baron, Sir Nigel Barkham-Twist (pronounced 'Bassett'), chairman of Media Moves International Inc., who also happens to be proprietor of their local paper, *The Witchester Echo* (*ster Echo*).

Sir Nigel is a local lad, who started business in Witchester back in 1934 with his own small publishing company, Barkham-Twist's (pronounced Bassett's), producing such notable titles as *Open That Boutique!*, the first in a series of business guides for the gifted homosexual, as well as the classic travel work *2000 Miles With a Bogey on My Lip* by Col. James R. Q. Pinder, and *My Life With Elvis* by Archbishop Desmond Tutu.

Thereafter, the business expanded rapidly. He founded *The Witchester Echo* in 1951, and during the years that followed started up dozens of similar enterprises all over the country. Nowadays, Sir Nigel controls several major news-

---

[1] 'What is it?'

Q: *Well, I thought kidnapping was illegal.*

Yes, it is. But if you get caught, it doesn't matter, because once you take over the running of the country, you'll be able to grant yourself an official pardon and walk out of prison a free man. So stop worrying.

Q: *But I don't want to go to prison in the first place. This is incitement to kidnapping! We're all going to be locked up! Oh my God!!*

For goodness' sake, quit whingeing . . .

Q: *Please don't do it.*

Shut up! I have to get back to the text . . .

paper titles in countries as far-flung as Wales and Scotland. Indeed, his control has recently been flung as far as Africa, Australia and Scandinavia too. Besides that, he has majority shareholdings in at least five British commercial radio stations, three soft drinks bottling plants, two vegan abattoirs, a string of launderettes in Heligoland and his own airline, and has just recently put in a bid for the top half of Andrew Lloyd Webber.

In short, Sir Nigel Barkham-Twist is a Very Big Cheese indeed.

And because the computer at the offices of *The Witchester Echo* is linked directly to the central database of Media Moves International in New York, Jeff realises that, by capitalising on Jeff Jnr's unique hacking skills, they can log into it and use this tiny, almost insignificant outpost in Sir Nigel's global communications empire as a means of intelligence-gathering for Terror Firma's operations worldwide.

Now, admittedly, the words 'Intelligence' and '*Witchester Echo*' are seldom mentioned in the same breath since, by even the most generous estimates, it's a toxic little rag full of showbiz tittle-tattle, blatant untruths about flash-in-the-pan celebrities, and photos of local May Queens with tits twice the size of Californian melons. Naturally, the whole paper is scorned and castigated by right-thinking people everywhere, who nevertheless read it in their tens of thousands.

You must have seen something similar on your local news-stands: those sleazy little tabloids carrying headlines such as, 'Postmistress, 67, chased and bitten by statue'; 'I was raped by Champion, the Wonder Horse – Exclusive' and '110-year-old blind and deaf crippled mute cleared of assault'. Plus, every Friday, it comes with a free pull-out called 'Siesta', aimed at brain-dead menopausal housewives who have managed to rear their children up to drug-taking age, and now just want to sit back and relax with a sixteen-page supplement that says nothing, does nothing, means nothing, and which is full of the most vacuous bollocks you've ever read in your life, including:

'*Dear Nadia*' – all your personal, emotional and sexual problems solved by a popular Romanian gymnast.

PLUS a 'sensational' free-to-enter competition: top prize is a weekend for one in a suburb of Rotterdam, whilst the first fifty runners-up will receive a street-map of Luton and a tea-towel with a rather fuzzy picture of Beethoven on it.

PLUS a special once-in-a-lifetime offer inviting readers to buy items of bankrupt stock, including a number of redundant souvenirs for the Prince Charles and Marie-Astrid Royal Wedding, some half-pint tankards with 'I voted for President Dukakis' on them, several hundred 'Free Zsa Zsa Gabor' car-stickers, and thousands of 'Beatles Reunion Concert 1982' T-shirts.

PLUS 'Three more tokens in our fabulous "Win-A-Pig" Offer!'

PLUS 'Star Burst', your horoscope for the week ahead written by somebody called Kosmic Kirsty, whose real name is Vera-Kay Burton and who works at the furniture shop in the precinct. Kosmik Kirsty is a true disciple of astrologer Russell Grant, to the extent that she copies his column word for word each week from the back of *Woman's Own*. Despite this, she has become quite a celebrity around town, thanks to the eerie accuracy of her predictions. For instance, at the age of nineteen she foretold that she would one day work in a furniture shop. Uncanny.

PROJECT VANESSA IS GO!!
Time, then, to nobble that tycoon.

After weeks of administrative foreplay – preparing plans, checking details of security within the MMI building, finding out where the victim's head office is, what his engagements are for the immediate future and so on – the Abercorns are all set to capture him and indoctrinate him with the principles of Faitheism.

(Incidentally, most of this private information is found out by Jeff Jnr when he hacks into Sir Nigel's personal file on the MMI central computer. In fact, it is the *only* way of finding it out, because the Abercorns will certainly get no joy from his secretary, Miss Quigley.

A secretary's role is to act as a blockade and prevent you from seeing her boss. To do this, she will use the stock fobbing-off phrases: 'I'm sorry, he's in a meeting right now, can I take a message?'; 'He's on the other line. Can I get him to call you back?'; 'Sir Nigel isn't at his desk at the moment, but I'll tell him you rang'; – without ever realising that we all grew wise to these infantile tricks years ago. But it means that her full and generous co-operation in the abduction process is by no means assured.)

Timing is crucial with all such missions: it must be a quick in-and-out operation, carefully planned and executed to a split-second schedule. Obviously, circumstances vary depending on the individual you plan to nobble, but here, as a step-by-step guide to help you, is how Jeff's plan is put into action.

Stage 1) *Penetration*
Posing as wholesalers of bathroom fittings on their delivery round, the C.L.I.T. members invade the London office of Media Moves International Inc., making their way swiftly to Sir Nigel's office on the top floor.

They have brought with them a key figure in this operation: Mr Cheesley, former owner of the Cafe Come Home in its pre-Rectum days, and previously a fully-qualified dentist. He was also a lay magistrate for a while – that is, until he was caught laying another magistrate in the car-park behind Witchester Co-Op, after which he was not only forced to retire from the bench, but was struck off from his dental practice as well. Even so, he is vital to the success of Project Vanessa.

Stage 2) *Keeping it up*
Once outside Sir Nigel's office, the C.L.I.T. unit members are dispersed as follows: Roz, Steph 1 and Bevs 5 to 7 keeping watch, covering the lifts and exits; three more Bevs quietly disposing of Sir Nigel's secretary, Miss Quigley; Steph 2 and Lesbo-in-Chief Lucette positioned outside Sir Nigel's office-door waiting for a sign from Mr Cheesley that he is ready to

go; and finally, Bev 4 standing to one side, well out of the way, operating the cassette-recorder.[2]

At this point, with Mr Cheesley and the others in position, Lucette punches Roz in the mouth three times – the signal to begin – and Steph 2 kicks in Sir Nigel's door.

An important point to note: As you burst in on your victim, the element of surprise is on your side, so don't do anything rash. Don't, for example, leap through the door of his office and start stabbing him with a potato-peeler – or even punching him with your fist. For a start, he won't like it. But also if, by chance, you happen to hurt him, he may prove somewhat unco-operative from this point on.

Bare-knuckle fighting is terribly crude anyway, and what works for the A-Team won't necessarily always pay off for a gang of ten lesbians posing as wholesalers of bathroom fittings. In the right situation, knuckles make the ideal weapon – they're light and, above all, easy to carry – so if they're the first thing that comes to hand, go ahead and use them. Otherwise, find an alternative.

Stage 3) *Climax*
Sir Nigel is stripped naked at Lucette's request and fixed to the wall with insulation tape, whilst Mr Cheesley injects him with 10ml of an intravenous barbiturate called Hypnoven.[3]

---

[2] This is text-book stuff. Once again, it pays to think about what a raid like this will look like if they turn your life-story into a movie. Ambushing a media tycoon in his own office in broad daylight could well be the high-point of the early part of the story. And no high-point in a film, whether it's a battle, a chase or a damned good nobbling like this one, is complete unless it is accompanied by enough stirring, all-action music to fill half a soundtrack album. Which is why you will need someone standing by throughout the entire raid, ready to turn the music up or down as when things get exciting. As I say, text-book stuff.

[3] Manufactured by Vierdrucker Industries mbH of Ambleburg, W. Germany, Hypnoven comes in three sizes: small, family and interrogation size. It is a drug used by dentists to induce heavy sedation in their patients. When the victim regains consciousness after a few minutes, he forgets instantly everything that has happened to him. It's a remarkable, if somewhat pointless, invention.

Anyone under the influence of the drug becomes particularly vulnerable to hypnotic suggestion. Therefore, any command, repeated over and over again, will sink deep into his subconscious mind, causing him to act automatically upon it, unable to distinguish between his own ideas and those that have been planted in his brain.

Suggestions like these are powerful little buggers. Once in place, they are impossible to shoo from the victim's mind and act as a sort of computer program, controlling his thoughts and actions from then on.

Therefore, whilst Sir Nigel is delirious, Lucette steps up and instructs him that, from now on, he will offer free advertising space to The Most Unholy Church of St Thomas the Doubter and to the Healthruherbs Compleat Health Plan in all of his newspapers and journals worldwide, as well as ensuring that any editorial coverage given to the Abercorns' activities in these publications is never anything but favourable.

That's all. But it should ensure that, as these instructions trickle down to the farthest corners of Sir Nigel's empire, his millions of customers in dozens of countries across the globe will be educated slowly into the ways of Faitheism and will accept it as more sensible and dependable than the religions which they have adopted to date but which have thoroughly duped and disappointed them all their lives.

Stage 4) *Withdrawal*

Job almost done, but there is one last matter to attend to before they leave: the Orgy Snap!

All members of the C.L.I.T. unit peel off their clothes and drape themswelves around Sir Nigel's body while Lucette takes an instant photo of them. This is their insurance policy in case, when he eventually does come round, he is able to remember even the teensiest bit of what has happened and is tempted to alert the authorities.

On the back of the photo is written the message: 'One word about this to anyone, you rich git, and we send a copy to *The News Of The World* – got that??' and it is left in a prominent place on Sir Nigel's desk.

Stage 5) *Cleaning the sheets*

Mission completed, the C.L.I.T. unit and Mr Cheesley pile into the bathroom-fittings van and speed away back to the Badger's Rectum for a celebratory glass of Jeff's homemade spinach sherry and a piping hot slice of dangleberry pie.

But hold on! Before you go around celebrating too much, don't forget that this is only half the task. Not only do all the world's other major media moguls have to be nobbled in the same way, but other branches of the media must be infiltrated as well – particularly TV and radio stations up and down the country. Their audiences will need to be hypnotised as soon as possible into supporting your world domination campaign.

Before we deal with all of this, however, perhaps we ought to let Jeff explain a few ways in which the media distort the truth and deceive us.

Jeff.

Jeff says . . .

'Day after day, from womb to tomb, we are bombarded with media-messages, screaming at us from hoardings, shop-windows, newspapers, magazines, TV and radio – tag-lines, trade-names, eye-catching pictures, mind-numbing slogans, urging us to buy a bigger this, a better that, a more magnificent the other; telling us what is good or bad for us, what is up-to-date or out of fashion, always selling, telling, compelling . . .

'Commercials entice you all the time into buying more and more, but seldom do they reveal anything like the whole truth about the products themselves.

'For example, how many chocolate bars have you eaten which, according to the ad, were filled with goodness, lashings of full-cream milk, nougat and sugar, and which made a jolly tasty snack between meals? Probably hundreds! But would you have bought them if the commercial had also told you that chocolate rots your teeth, can make you fat and spotty, may cause kidney stones or spark off diabetes and could be a major cause of stomach cancer?

'Of course not.

'Similarly, if the next can of paint you bought contained a warning that the company which manufactured it was one of the major polluters of seas and rivers in the world, would you ever go for that brand again?

'Of course not.

'And manufacturers know this. But rather than admit to what they are really up to, they prefer to sit tight and keep quiet, using expensive commercials and clever PR to gloss over the truth, in the hope that nobody will uncover what is really going on.

'By way of a for-instance, let's run through some of the tag-lines most commonly used to sell products or services, and find out what the phrases actually mean.

Restaurants

Home-made – We poured it out of the can and heated it up ourselves

Farmhouse recipe – We made it from a powder

Fresh – Well, yes, it was fresh when we bought it over a week ago . . .

Freshly squeezed orange-juice – Freshly squeezed out of a carton, that is, not out of an orange!

Shops and supermarkets

Special offer – We're desperate, please buy one

10% bigger – The wrapper's 10% bigger, not the contents

Bigger and better than ever – They've redesigned the packet

Two for the price of one – It's not selling and they've got a warehouse full of the stuff, so they're resorting to bribery to shift their stocks

50% extra *free* – Business is bad, the bailiffs have been called in, so now they're giving it away

A never-to-be-repeated offer – We've gone into liquidation

With special free gift – We've bought a huge consignment of the cheapest load of old tat we could lay our hands on, and now we want you to have it

Probably the best – But it isn't

Tastes better than ever – It was crap before, now it's just disgusting

Product guaranteed – i.e. It's guaranteed to break down only after the guarantee has run out

Longer lasting – Than what, though? Igneous rock maybe? A trip to Venus? The life-cycle of a protozoa? They don't say. Nor will they ever, because it's utterly meaningless

Experts recommend it . . . – . . . mind you, all the experts work for us, so they were bound to like it, I suppose

Full of natural goodness – It probably contains a dozen chemicals – don't touch it

From Mother Nature's larder – It most definitely contains chemicals – don't touch it

It tastes like the cake grandmother used to bake – If your grandmother baked cakes using base metals, artificial flavourings and ten or more preservatives and colourings, then yes, it no doubt tastes exactly like the one she used to bake

100% meat – That depends on how you define meat really. In all cases, look carefully at the list of ingredients. You'll find it probably contains pig's knackers, crushed budgerigars, a couple of old Grand National winners, the bits of a sheep that even vets don't get to see, plus several odds and ends from dead dogs that are so stale and disgusting they daren't even put them in pork sausages!

Newspaper advertisements and features

A million copies sold . . . – . . . by us to the shops, who haven't been able to get rid of a single one

Money refunded if not completely satisfied – Always provided you can be bothered to stick it back in the box, wrap it up, tie it with string, carry it to the post office, post it and wait two months for us to reply, then sure, bud, we'll give you your money back

A one-off gift lovingly produced just for you – By a machine in Taiwan that churns out 10,000 a day. It's a con

A million pounds to be won – i.e. a million people will receive a pound each. Another con

Win the house of your dreams absolutely free – Con deluxe! It is just a crafty way of selling home-insurance, but even if it's not, you have more chance of being picked to play soccer for England or of winning the Cheltenham Gold Cup without a horse, than you have of ever receiving the keys to that coveted dream-house

'In short, everyone is out to deceive everyone else, so why should we be any different? You must be prepared to spread the word of Faitheism in any way you can and if that means playing a little dirty occasionally, well so be it.

'Don't let scruples get in the way of a job well done.'

Thanks, Jeff.

He's right about the brainwashing. We're all subject to this battering by the media for most of our lives, so it must be clear by now what powerful tools TV and radio will be once they are working to promote your cause. Of course, it stands to reason that no respectable broadcasting station is going to help you openly with your plan, so once again, you will have to be all sneaky and resort to backdoor methods. And this is what we'll deal with next.

Practical Exercise: Taking Control of a Radio Station

Codename: Project Corin

First of all, I want you to go back and take another look at page 64, and all that stuff we said about planting thoughts in a tycoon's subconscious mind while he was asleep.

Found it?

Good. Well, we're now going to do the same sort of thing again, only this time to millions of ordinary people by planting carefully-chosen subliminal messages into the output of every radio and TV station in the country.

Q: *Right. So let's get on with it, then.*

Fine.

PROJECT CORIN IS GO!!

Broadcasting twenty-four hours a day, Witch FM – 'The Big Noise in Wittie' – is the Abercorns' local independent radio station. It's no different to dozens of other stations around the country, pumping out a continuous incoherent blend of music by people who can't sing, chat by people who have nothing to say and competitions entered by people who think the capital of Norway is Vienna. Their daily output is hopelessly uneven, varying between 'really quite dire' when things aren't going well, and 'utterly abysmal' when they are.

Every other record is by Phil Collins – that's the station policy, and wherever possible the records in between them are by Phil Collins too. Any songs not sung by Phil Collins must be either produced by him or have him as guest drummer on them. In other words, it's music to Hoover to, punctuated every three minutes by adverts for cheap mortgages and car telephones, and presented by a host of grinning mindless androids who babble endlessly about how fabulous and brilliant and 'hey, hey, super' everything is, when it patently isn't, but if they didn't say it was they'd be sacked.

Jeff's plan, then, is to wheedle his way into Witch FM's studio complex and plant a cassette-recorder containing an endless loop-tape of subliminal messages inside a piece of electronic gadgetry called 'The Optimod'. This is a device which, like most other technical things, is fairly boring to look at and ten times as boring to describe. But to give you some idea . . .

Think of a tumble-dryer, okay?

Now think of the Arc de Triomphe in Paris.

And finally, think of a small metallic box with lots of little switches and knobs on the front.

Well, it's more like the small metallic box with lots of little switches and knobs on the front!

At its simplest, an Optimod is a small in-line unit which acts as a compressor, processing the signal from a radio or TV station before it is sent to the transmitter and broadcast to the audience. By doctoring the Optimod in a radio station, for example, and wiring up a cassette-recorder into the back of it, you can broadcast your subliminals directly to the station's listeners every day and nobody will be any the wiser.

That is the plan anyway, but before he can get at the Optimod, Jeff somehow has to penetrate the strict security system at the radio station, and I should imagine that this will probably be your main problem as well. How *do* you slip past the guards unseen?

Well, to my mind, there are two alternatives: either a) you turn up one afternoon unannounced and, without warning, unleash a wild, unfed puma into the foyer. Then, during the ensuing carnage, you nip swiftly past the security-man and slip into the building unseen.

Or, better still, b) gain access legitimately at the station's own invitation.

This is Jeff's favourite – it's simpler, less conspicuous and, besides, the puma has a throat infection and is down at the vet's.

So the next day, Suzuki is told to ask the careers teacher at her school, St Montelimar's School for Foreign-Looking Children, whether it would be possible for the whole class to take a fabulous and brilliant and hey-hey-super educational trip around Witch FM's studios in Witchester.

The radio station will have no choice but to agree to this. They won't want to, of course. In fact, it's bloody inconvenient all round. Broadcasters hate meeting the public at the best of times; they regard their listeners as dim-witted and troublesome and feel that the station would be much better off without them. However, a tour is good for PR and it also gives them the chance to flog thousands of cheap stickers, mugs and badges which they bought a year ago and which are still clogging up nine shelves, two lockers and a cupboard in the stockroom.

Once inside the station, the party is led to the Master Control Room, or 'MastContRoo' for short. Or 'MCR' for evenshorterstill.

Suzuki bides her time and waits for the right moment when the whole class is distracted, watching Witch FM's top DJ Billy 'Hey-Hey-Super' Divine on air, as he tries to explain to the listeners exactly who The Beatles were. Then, when no-one is looking, she slopes off quietly to find the Optimod device.

After unscrewing its front panel, and following Jeff Jnr's instructions to the letter, she pulls out the whole unit to about four inches, slips the cassette-player into the back, wires it into the power source and the limiting circuit, then screws the unit back into place and runs off to rejoin the class.

Clever girl! Not like her at all really.

From this point onwards, whenever people listen to Witch FM, they will receive not only the regular transmissions, but also, without realising it, the constant stream of subliminal messages about Faitheism as well. These messages are inaudible, so listeners won't pick them up consciously, only subconsciously. But if they are repeated over and over again, day in, day out, they will slip unnoticed into their minds, brainwashing them into supporting the cause and, when the time comes, voting the Abercorns into power as well.

72

To give you an example of how it works, on the left below is what you would *actually* hear if you tuned in to Witch FM, whilst on the right are some of the subliminal messages that you wouldn't hear, but which your subconscious mind would pick up as you were listening.

What you hear	*What you hear subliminally*
On 98.5, this is Witch FM, I'm Billy Divine, with you between now and three, and I'll be playing the best music around, hit after hit after hit – hey, hey, super! And Mrs Jill Tinker writes from Wittie – she wants something by Jason Donovan please, for her disabled daughter Christine, who she says has just come out of hospital after a serious leg operation. She's in the most terrible pain, says Jill, but a song by her favourite star Jason would really cheer her up. Well, I'm sorry, Christine, but we don't play shit like that on this show. So here's Phil Collins singing the old Applejacks number, 'Tell Me When'. Hey, hey . . . super!	I believe that there is no external God-force; I am a free-thinking individual, able to make my own decisions; I am self-sufficient; I go my own way; I do not respect the authority of any government; I am free; I think for myself; Religion bores the pants off me; I am a true Faitheist; I am liberated from all my responsibilities to society; I do everything according to my own thoughts, plans and ideas; I value my freedom and shun authority of any kind; I am a pilot in my life and not a passenger; I believe in my own abilities; I want to help take over the world – just tell me when.

Of course, to some of you it may seem like pie-in-the-sky, all of this. But you should never underestimate the devastating power of subliminals. Used correctly, they can topple governments, win wars, change a whole nation's attitude and turn millions of people around in their thinking and beliefs, simply by tampering with their subconscious minds.

Take it from me, subliminals are big heavy *powerful* stuff. Otherwise, why would they be banned?

4

Stirring Up Trouble Abroad

It is clear that Jeff, as Archbishop of the Most Unholy Church of St Thomas the Doubter, needs to spread the message of Faitheism to foreign lands in double-quick time if he is to meet the World Domination deadline of one year. In particular, he must introduce it into a large number of unstable countries in Africa and the Middle East where other religions currently have the upper hand.

In such places, the people have traditionally been raised on the idea of one loving, caring God who, in spite of their constant prayers to Him, nevertheless seems happy to let them be bombed, shelled and machine-gunned non-stop for years on end by their enemies. So much so, that they are beginning to wonder whether all that stuff they were taught as kids about the Almighty Father always watching over them and protecting them wasn't a bit overstated after all, and maybe even a con-trick – thus making them perfect targets for conversion to Faitheism.

To effect the conversion, Jeff decides to appoint a special envoy, a charismatic trouble-shooter to oversee the Church's continued expansion overseas.

WHAT A SPECIAL ENVOY DOES
Don't worry about the fancy title. A special envoy's job is simple and involves: a) maintaining a high profile in South America, South Africa and the Middle East, pleading for the release of all political prisoners and crouching in huddles with moustachioed bandits, while women in veils run around in the background with babies, dodging masonry and overhead power-cables as they drop into the streets;

b) striking up bargains with kidnappers and gun-men in Beirut – most of whom will probably be aged ten years or younger – for the release of longer-term hostages. Armed children are bastards to negotiate with, though, and exactly how many packets of M&Ms or rolls of Postman Pat wallpaper they will accept in return for each hostage is anybody's guess!;

c) addressing guerrilla leaders and helping them to hatch complex schemes which, on paper at least, make it look as though lifelong rifts between warring factions are finally being healed once and for all, but which will allow both sides to keep on killing each other indefinitely if things don't work out;

d) flying backwards and forwards, meddling, bullying and conniving until the rival factions get so pissed off with his neverending interference that they take him hostage as well!

NB. If your special envoy is not kidnapped on the first visit, then he must return again and again until he is. That way, he will vanish for months on end, maybe even years if you're lucky, generating lots of excitement in diplomatic circles – the sort of excitement which suggests that the government is doing something to help the situation, when in fact the diplomats are just overjoyed at the thought of appearing on hourly news bulletins as they push through a forest of microphones and cameras, muttering, 'No comment. No, no. I have nothing to say. Sorry.'

NNB. There is no room for sentimentality here either. You must never become too attached to your envoy. Don't forget, this is a media war we're fighting, and any kidnapping of this sort will receive acres of daily publicity of the sort that money simply can't buy. Regular peak air-time on TV will heighten awareness of your cause amongst ABC1 category viewers, and should rake in thousands of recruits to your Church as a result, so try to be objective. If your envoy is held captive by terrorists, try to look upon him less as a hostage, more as a gift. They can keep him – you've got plenty more where he came from.

On the other hand if, by sheer bad luck, things go horribly wrong and he is released unexpectedly, then make sure you do the right thing: give him a stage-managed 'welcome-home' party, parade him before the press, make him answer any questions they pose about his captors, the state of his cell, etc, and then, when the fuss begins to die down, simply pack him off back to the Middle East again to be recaptured.

The question is, though: whom should Jeff appoint to this coveted and prestigious post?

Well, as on previous occasions, he is not afraid to stick his neck out and make good use of the disenfranchised minorities who have taken shelter at 17, Campbell Avenue and its neighbouring houses. So, after much deliberation and discussion, he eventually appoints Mr Carmichael, the tramp from the precinct – the one who kips in Halford's doorway and makes his money by dead-legging window-shoppers and running off with their handbags. He is shrewd, alert and above all, he understands the streets. After all, he's slept in most of them.

KEY PERSONNEL PROFILE 6:
MR CARMICHAEL, SPECIAL ENVOY

Duggie Carmichael is a jolly, colourful character, very popular with the locals in the town.

Smelling strongly of urine, not all of it his own, and with a large tattoo of Valerie Singleton across his forehead, which he had done on impulse after a particularly stimulating edition of 'The Money Programme', he was recently voted 'Down'n'Out of the Year' by the Witchester Shop Doorways Maintenance Association.

Mr Carmichael is the kind of person who gives alcoholism and extreme drug abuse a bad name, and he knows it, often admitting that, were it not for his pathological weakness for strong ale and smokes, his life might have shown a better return all round. For a start, he wouldn't have got rat-arsed on Pernod one night last June and lost his labouring job at the Gardening Centre for the Partially Illiterate (motto: 'If we can't spell it, we don't sell it' – for that reason alone, secateurs were always out of stock, and they never sold Rhododendrons either, or Gladioli, Azaleas, several brands of compost, or any one of a hundred flowering shrubs with impossible Latin names).

Duggie joined the army for a while in the early seventies, amid startling rumours that he was Scottish – a slur he somehow never managed to shake off. At the time, he was married with two children and living in a converted two-up-two-down in South Witchester, a happy family man – much the same as his closest friend and drinking companion, Vince 'Donkey-Dick' Osmond, who was at one time long ago a crossword compiler for *The Guardian* newspaper. He had a wife too, and a baby, and they lived in a three-down six-across in Bishop's Stortford. Now, however, twenty years on, both men are hopeless alcoholics, divorced, destitute, unemployable and idyllically pissed most of the time, which, dipso facto, means they are of no use whatsoever to society.

Even so, you should never misjudge a man like this. He is streetsmart, a real shrewd cookie who could be of enormous value to you in your fight against the System. There are no flies on Mr Carmichael – at least, not as many as there used to be.

Sure, he may look dirty, disgusting, fetid and old. But strip away his soiled overcoat and the filthy mackintosh underneath, and the three threadbare jackets, and the carcoat with no sleeves, the waterproof overtrousers, legliners, four lumberjack shirts, seven vests, two scarves, Pacamac, cravat, cummabund, those chocolate-brown Y-fronts that were white when he put them on, his Oxfam waistcoat, the jolly rainbow tanktop he nicked from Benetton last winter, his parka, corduroy jump-suit, black velveteen nightdress, toreador cape, snorkelling outfit, waders, sports socks, undersocks, oversocks, longjohns, balaclava, snood, pantyhose, jodhpurs, cycling shorts, rainhood, kilt and mocassins; then detoxify him, descale his teeth, cut his hair, give him a pedicure, manicure, cold-cure, liver operation and possibly an autopsy just to be on the safe side; shave him, bathe him, shampoo him, delouse him, scrub and disinfect him, hose him down, roll him in oatmeal, rinse him and talc him and leave him to simmer over a warm heat for twenty minutes; then, finally, towel him thoroughly and wrap him in a thick bathrobe . . . and he's just like you and me.

All he asks for is compassion, understanding and a chance to begin again. With any luck, holding the post of Archbishop Abercorn's special envoy will give him that chance. It means he is a man of the cloth. Of course, that doesn't make him a saint or a saviour or a miracle worker. He can't turn water into wine, for instance. Although his trick of turning cider into urine is still a sight worth seeing!

Mr Carmichael may be grossly inarticulate at times, but this can only be an asset when dealing with senior churchmen. Couple it with his profligate use of the F-word, to such an extent that even Bob Geldof would wince with embarrassment, and you can understand why Jeff thinks he is ideal for religious duties – meeting stuffy, pompous, old-fashioned, self-righteous clergymen and cutting them down to size. There is no doubt about it, when it comes to scaring the shit out of church leaders, Mr Carmichael has the Midas touch.

And that goes for the Pope too. Mr Carmichael may never be Primate himself, but most of his closest relatives are primates, which makes him a popular choice for the job.

So within a matter of days, Duggie Carmichael, the perfect candidate, is dispatched to Beirut to take up his post as Archbishop Abercorn's special envoy. We can check on his progress a little later.

Mr Carmichael hits it off with the Bishop of Durham.

5

The Men In Grey Suits Fight Back

Of course, it's all very well starting religions and organising terrorist cells and rallying the disenfranchised minorities to the clarion call of freedom and justice, but if you plan to introduce sweeping political and religious change and become a major world figure, then The Men In Grey Suits, those stuffy officious bureaucrats whose job it is to keep things precisely the way they are, will be none too impressed with the idea, you can be sure of it.

The Men In Grey Suits are paid to keep the status as quo as possible, which means they usually take to radical change like a duck takes to a microwave. Consequently, if you go too far and things get out of hand, they will have no alternative but to put a stop to your little efforts as soon as possible. To their mind, folk-heroes like yourself are fine, so long as they remain just that: folk-heroes – jumped-up variety entertainers who are here today, still here tomorrow, but gone the day after that. Anything more and they're dangerous. Anything more than dangerous, and very soon they're not just folk-heroes, they're *dead* ones.

The secret of success in this game, therefore, is to keep a low profile. Don't let on to anyone what you're up to. Trust nobody. Always discuss your plans in private at the dead of night with the lights off, preferably under a thick quilt. And even then, only communicate in whispers. Don't forget, voices carry. 'Walls have sausages,' as Mrs Greenhalgh is prone to saying, in her robust but lovable West Country way.

If you don't keep your intentions to yourself and The Men

81

In Grey Suits catch a whiff of what you're up to, things could get just a little sticky.

Q: *Exactly how sticky?*

Difficult to say really, but 'very very very' is not far off the mark, I should think.

To begin with, you may become the target of covert enquiries by MI5, the British national security service, and maybe even MI6, the international intelligence agency. It is even possible that MFI could become involved too, although come to think of it, this is unlikely since they're a chain of discount furniture warehouses. Then no doubt members of the CIA, the American intelligence network who, by all accounts, have their grubby fingers in lots of highly dubious pies overseas, will start sniffing around. After that, there is Interpol and the Swiss National Guard and a myriad others, all curious about what you're up to, who are bound to come snooping around in the hope of picking up odd snippets of information.

Therefore, the message here is: be prepared. If you're not, it is impossible to overstate how unpleasant things could become for you, although a big sub-heading done in heavy print should give you some sort of indication.

UNPLEASANTNESS

It happens on two levels: what we'll call 'The Worrying Level' and 'The Messy Level'.

FIRST OF ALL, THE WORRYING LEVEL

That's right. Nothing too spectacular to begin with, just a spot of low-profile surveillance during the first few weeks, to see what you're about.

a) Phone-tapping

Some things are sent to try us – judges and juries, for instance. And phone-tapping is another.

You can almost guarantee that your phone-calls will be monitored closely at some time during Operation Redgrave, and probably sooner rather than later. According to recent statistics, 21,000 private telephone lines in Britain were tapped in 1987.[4] Common eavesdropping, that's all it is, but standard procedure for The Men In Grey Suits.

The days when a secret agent in a dapper Burberry's raincoat with the collar turned up, would hover conspicuously under a streetlamp, lighting cigarette after cigarette as he watched your bedroom window from across the road, are long gone. Things have changed radically. Many detectives have quit smoking for a start, or else switched to cocaine. On top of which, some of them are getting quite old now and need to sit down while they work, and so are more likely to monitor your comings and goings from an anonymous grey van with blacked-out windows, parked two doors along from your home.

Usually, though, this tiresome round-the-clock vigil will have been assigned to some weary young graduate, fresh from college, who is serving his or her three-month assessment period by listening in on totally innocent everyday conversations, looking for morsels of treachery and giveaway signs indicating that the country is about to be overrun by subversives at any minute. It may not be the easiest way to earn a living, but for these people, barely out of their teens yet already cynical and bored with life, it is a convenient, hassle-free excuse to while away forty years in public service, until they are pensioned off at fifty-five with a gold carriage-clock and a bullet through the stomach,[5] as a gentle reminder to them not to try publishing their memoirs after they leave.

The surveillance agents will assume that you must be a Commie subversive right from the start, and work back from there. Trouble is, these chaps spend so much time stewing in nationalistic paranoia that they are quite capable of reading treacherous motives into even the simplest of statements,

[4] Figures courtesy of Concoctastat Ltd.
[5] It is generally recognised that anyone who has spent forty years listening in to other people's conversations must know too much about what is going on in the world and is best disposed of before they can tell anyone. An engraved bullet is the quickest way, and is known in Establishment circles as a Mafia Handshake.

and could construe the average grocery list as a serious threat to Western democracy and the stability of NATO.

So you have only to let slip with some jokey off-the-cuff comment – something innocuous such as 'Hey, I've had a great idea. Let's nuke Paris!!' – and immediately they'll read all manner of dark meaning into it. That's their job. That's the way they are.

Alas, you will find it exceedingly difficult to tell whether your phone is being tapped or not – there may be a steady clicking occasionally as you speak, or a high-pitched peeping-sound whenever you make or take a call. Alternatively, there could be a slight echo, as though you're talking into a deep electronic well, and once in a while you might even catch a far-off suppressed sneeze, or somebody shouting, 'Hey, Gerry, fetch us two onion bhajis and a Kit-Kat, will ya?' – that kind of thing. But frequently, there is nothing at all to give the game away.

So to be on the safe side, you should take evasive action as soon as possible, a few simple precautions: 1) make all secret calls from a mobile telephone positioned as far from the nearest cell-site as possible. Calls cannot be monitored unless there is a scanning receiver nearby, so if you constantly change location, you will be untraceable;

2) when using your home-phone, always scramble the call. This is now standard practice in the Abercorn household, so that, on the odd occasion when Fidel Castro calls Mrs Greenhalgh (very old buddies, these two – they go way back, both sharing a deep lust for power, as well as an unparalleled fascination with the music of The Applejacks), Julie Hoovers continuously nearby, whilst Suzuki plays 'By the Rivers of Babylon' on her Stylophone close to the mouthpiece.

Scramble that call!

Alternatively, why not invent a system of code-phrases which can be worked into everyday conversations and which would warn the caller to 'beware – phone-tapping in progress'.

For example, the phrase, 'I have a haemorrhoid and am incapable of cycling right now' could mean 'This line is being tapped, I'll give you a call later from a public phone-box.' To

which the caller might reply, 'You have a spider in your hair
. . . Hey, what a great title for a song!' which means, 'Okay,
I'll be in for the next thirty minutes, then I'm going to Tescos
to buy some aubergines and four low-fat yoghurts. Speak to
you soon.'

But that is not all. You may also find that your mail goes
astray, or that letters arrive completely shredded, or opened
and mysteriously sealed back down again, or that they are
delivered three to four years after they were posted. Of
course, in Witchester, it is hard to distinguish this from
the normal postal service, but if it happens to you, take
it as a clear message that your letters have somehow
been intercepted along the way and the contents photo-
graphed.

b) One of your operatives goes missing

The scenario: Suzuki is riding her bicycle up and down
Campbell Avenue when a black Mercedes skids up to the
kerb, two thugs leap out, concuss her fiercely with a
breeze-block, and drag her inside. The car screeches away
and disappears off in the direction of Southampton.

Suzuki has been abducted!!

Whew! Lucky it wasn't somebody important, eh?

If they'd nabbed the right person, one of the Cheeslies, or
even Julie or Jeff Jnr, this could have been a dangerous
broadside on the Abercorns' whole operation. Before long,
swarms of Flying Squad detectives or CIA men could descend
on the Badger's Rectum, brandishing warrants and revolvers
and half-eaten onion bhajis and maps showing the precise
location of the secret tunnel leading to Sea View . . . Hell, it
doesn't bear thinking about!

But fortunately, Suzuki knows next to nothing, and what
she does know she doesn't understand, so everything is okay.

The Men In Grey Suits will take her to a secret place such as
a dingy basement office, after which, who knows what horrors
they will inflict upon her poor, frail, quasi-Japanese body?
She could be made to drink a gallon of scalding hot water, or,
worse, she could be forced to sit through endless reruns of
The Partridge Family until she finally breaks down and

submits to high-pressure questioning about Faitheism and the activities of Terror Firma.

Once they have all the information they need, they will inject her with Sodium Pentathol to make her forget all that has happened, before tapping her generously about the face and shoulders with a cricket bat, pushing her back into the Mercedes and running it into a passing tree to make it look like an accident.

The lesson here, therefore, is: . . . well, I'm not quite sure really . . . although it's probably: 'Don't tell Suzuki any more than she needs to know.' But also, try and ensure that you have more than one child, just in case you lose one during your ongoing fight for freedom and enlightenment.

c) Infiltration by secret agents
There are various methods used by the big national intelligence networks to gather vital information about you:

i) *'Sigint'*. Short for 'signal intelligence' – intercepting transmissions broadcast from overseas by the strategic use of satellites, ground-based dishes and even fishing-trawlers laced with antennae moored off the coast of North-West Scotland, as they shadow the movements of foreign naval fleets in the North Sea and monitor transmissions by Russian agents working out of Ullapool;

ii) *'Elint'*. Electronic intelligence – bugging, tapping, rapping, knocking, kicking, screaming, walnutting, etc;

iii) *'Humint'*. Human intelligence – that is to say, having an agent out on the ground, doing investigations, interviews, tailing people around, peering nervously through their letterbox, etc – James Bond type stuff;

iv) *'Peergint'*. Sub-human intelligence – keeping a close watch on members of the House of Lords in case they wake up or move unexpectedly.

Now, there is nothing to say that this intelligence-collection process has to be all one way. You may feel like turning the tables and sending out a unit of your own to keep tabs on what The Men In Grey Suits themselves are up to.

Make no mistake, though, bureaucrats are always on the ball. And for every insurgence squad you may have, the intelligence service will have a corresponding counter-insurgence squad. Similarly, for every anti-counter-insurgence unit you put together, you can be sure that the government will train up one of their contra-anti-counter-insurgence squads. Taking it one stage further. If you are keen to outwit them, you may feel the need to form a discontra-anticounterinsurgence squad. Well, fine, do it. But you may well discover before too long that the other side fully expected this to happen anyway, and already have an undiscontra-anticounterinsurgence squad of their own to foil your plan.

In short, whatever happens, it is highly likely that The Men In Grey Suits will be way ahead of the game and will try to find out even more information about you by infiltrating your organisation.

This may be done covertly or really quite conspicuously. For instance, not so long ago, a stranger turned up at the Abercorns' home, claiming to be a Mr Peter Malpas from Allied Mould and Rot, and saying he wanted to examine their damp course for signs of radiation. He had a swish ID card and a little black bag with odd bits of transmitting equipment and a small generator in it, and seemed to know what he was doing, so they let him get on with the job.

Over the next two hours, he made several checks, numerous notes, endless calculations, a series of short phone-calls – some of them to the USSR – and then sat on the sofa and refused to leave.

That was six months ago. And now, Jeff and the family are beginning to wonder if he isn't a spy.

'Is it or isn't it?'

THE MESSY LEVEL
If, after preliminary surveillance, you are thought by The Men In Grey Suits to be a group of Commie or Fascist extremists up to no good, and posing an immediate threat to national security,[6] they will have no choice but to put a stop to your activities immediately, and this they may do in a number of ways.

a) The Fake Break-in
Under the guise of an ordinary everyday household burglary, a handful of agents in balaclava helmets and Milletts anoraks will be dispatched from head office to break into your home or office while you are out.

They will ransack a few things, vandalise everything else, remove vital papers, plans, maps, sketches, photos, any detonators or grenades you've left carelessly lying around, as well as your VCR, your compact disc player – especially if it has a multi-play function with infra-red remote control – and some jewellery for their wives. All your pets will be fed with plastic explosives and then detonated, and your robust but lovable West Country housekeeper, if you have one, will be strung up from the ceiling in the hallway by a boathook.

Professionally-executed violence with damage to property, a vicious assault and some random gratuitous hooliganism thrown in, makes it look like a bona fide robbery and also provides them with a new video recorder for their common room. They work odd, unsociable hours, these people, and frequently miss their favourite soaps as a result. A new VCR will help them keep up with the storylines.

So what happens after this?

Well, next thing, you come home to find you've been

---

[6] An overworked catch-all phrase this. Generally speaking, it means that they believe you're going to do something pretty heavy soon, something that will upset the status quo and start spoiling things for everyone else, such as telling the people the Truth about what is really going on in the world. It therefore calls for emergency action. When this happens, you know you've hit the subversive jackpot, and you will begin to feel as though your whole life is caving in around you. Enjoy.

burgled. The break-in is reported to the police who turn up, ask dozens of questions, make notes, use your lavatory and go; then you claim everything back on your household insurance, and . . . well, that's that really. Case closed. The police rarely catch house-burglars anyway, and they most certainly won't want to arrest a member of the Yugoslavian Secret Service or SAS or UHT or whoever it turns out to be, by mistake, will they? So from their point of view, the sooner the matter is swept under the carpet and forgotten about the better.

If this happens to you, therefore, you should look on it as an early warning, a foretaste of what is to come when you really do become a global Messiah. Your best and easiest solution to the problem is to be prepared. Leave someone watching over the premises at all times, and make sure they are fully armed in the event of a surprise attack.

b) Waste-disposal

Some groups of people are seen as being beyond the ransacking stage, however.

They become such a threat to democracy, either by their actions or by what they know, that The Men In Grey Suits have precious little choice but to quietly and efficiently dispose of them. And this is where things can get a little scary. If ever you were considering giving up on the whole idea of ruling the world, then this is the point to quit.

For the benefit of all COAK addicts, here is another of Jeff's special Cut Out And Keep sections explaining how the government secrecy machine operates to protect itself.

91

Jeff says . . .

'The very worst thing that can happen to you in a modern Western democracy is for The Men In Grey Suits to brand you a "troublemaker".

'It's a technical term used in Establishment circles to describe anyone who, either accidentally or by persistent effort, has come uncomfortably close to finding out What Is Really Going On. If this happens and they do classify you as a spanner in their carefully-oiled works, then you are as good as dead already, and you may as well throw yourself off a bridge at your leisure rather than sit around waiting to be terminated by the authorities.

'The methods of retaliation at their disposal are frightening. False imprisonment, or having you beaten up and left half-dead outside your own front door, or even raiding your home under warrant and "finding" a small sachet of white powder which you would swear wasn't there before, and then arresting you for possession of it . . . it all adds up. And you are left in no doubt that you have finally been branded a troublemaker.

'The official punishment for treachery is thirty years' imprisonment, the unofficial punishment is a couple of busted kneecaps, multiple skull fractures and twenty-two weeks in hospital.

'In extreme circumstances, they will stop at nothing to shut you up. Let's face it, there are so many random and callous homicides these days, who is going to notice one more? Who will suspect skulduggery if you are involved in an unfortunate accident as you drive home from the office? Similarly, when the brakes fail on that juggernaut you're steering around a tricky corner halfway down a perilous mountain pass . . . the truck jack-knifes off the road and tumbles in a flaming twisted wreck down to the slate-quarry below, with you sitting dead at the wheel . . . who would ever know that your brakes had been tampered with?

'Nobody, that's who.

'At this level, abuses of power and infringements of personal liberty go largely unchallenged. Whole jet-planes may be bombed or shot right out of the sky; ferry-boats may unaccountably capsize and sink, drowning everyone on board; cars will be involved in mysterious pile-ups on dual carriageways in thick fog . . . it goes on and on. Official reports classify them as accidents, pilot error, foolish motorists driving too fast in poor conditions, when what you are really witnessing is intelligence agencies from different countries slugging it out on a daily basis with subversive underworld factions, and killing each other indiscriminately in the process.

'You see, then, that there is a level, and it is a very high one admittedly, way above most people's experience, at which justice becomes a matter of pot luck, where the rules of fair play are non-existent and where you are on your own. At this point, it is just you versus the System. But at such a level, the state can do more or less as it pleases with you, and you are powerless to contest it. The rules, if there are any, become obscure, and The Men In Grey Suits gang together to cover their tracks with an outbreak of official amnesia until, as time goes by, your case is buried deep under a mountain of bureaucracy, ignored by a hierarchy of frightened individuals working frantically together to protect their own backs.

'Let me give you three imaginary for-instances where their work would be most obvious to outsiders such as ourselves:

'i) *For instance*, a successful actress becomes too "involved" with a major world leader to the point where their sexual liaison begins to jeopardise "national security" and she can no longer be trusted to keep her mouth shut. Before long, she is discovered in a motel room, alongside a bottle of Campari and an empty aspirin jar, having committed suicide apparently without reason.

'Naturally, the press have a field day. The young lady becomes a legend, films are made about her tragic life, books are written, mini-series are shot, all guessing at the reasons for her untimely demise. But nobody comes near to the truth.

'Of course, she hasn't really committed suicide, we all know that. This is death by committee. It has been done for her by some secret friends who called during the night and persuaded her that a painless death right there and then would have considerable pluses compared to what would happen to her if she refused.

'ii) *For instance*, the Pope dies, and another one is quickly elected to take his place. But this new Pope sees things differently from his predecessor. He wants to make big changes, changes that will affect the way the Vatican is run, relations with its close political allies, various organisations, world leaders and so on.

'Clearly, this simply won't do. So what happens?

'You can probably guess the rest. The poor old man passes away in his sleep – with more than a little inducement from some secret visitors to his rooms, who encourage him to visit the nearest cemetery and stay there. Needless to say, he is never seen or heard of again. Meantime, Roman Catholics the world over mourn the passing of the Primate. Soon after, a new Pope is appointed, the storm quickly passes and the whole incident is forgotten.

'iii) *For instance*, a former president of the United States is about to step on board a plane to Europe. At the last minute, a firm hand is placed on his shoulder and a knowing voice whispers in his ear, "Mr President, Sir, you must not board that plane. Come this way please."

94

'Sensing an urgency about the stranger's command, he relents and goes back through the departure gate. Several hours later, that same plane is mysteriously shot down while crossing Eastern Europe in a muddle over airspace restrictions. Several hundred innocent passengers die, the incident makes world headlines for days, but, like all such disasters, it soon becomes old news.

'However, the former president's life has been saved and nobody is any the wiser. Well, somebody is, but we never discover who!

'So be careful. You can't fight fire with fire in this game. Instead, you just have to be as devious as The Men In Grey Suits are, and then some. Above all, don't meddle in the shady world of international skulduggery, not unless you want to end up with your whole body filleted and dumped down a railway embankment, or you want to be washed up on the banks of the Solent with your private parts rammed halfway down your throat.'

Whew!!
Jeff can get pretty heavy at times, can't he?
But he's right, and that brings us, finally, to the worst category in our list of Unpleasantnesses:

c) The ultimate mess
There is one other punishment lying in wait for an unwanted outsider who tries to make an impact on world affairs. it is without doubt the most sinister and disastrous piece of unpleasantness of them all, but since it is unlikely to happen to you at such an early stage in your plans, we should perhaps stick it behind our ear for later, until we can deal with it in more detail and in its proper context.

Q: *All right, then. But what happens if the CIA or the KGB or whoever the hell else, decides to try and stop me taking over the world . . . what can I do about it?*

Excellent point.
In your unceasing drive for power over the whole of civilisation, there are some characters you would be well

advised to steer clear of. We know about The Men In Grey Suits, of course, but also on the list are the IRA, the PLO, the Catholic Church and the big South American drug cartels. I wouldn't tangle with the Moslems either, if I were you, or Devil-worshippers, spiritualists, Jehovah's Witnesses, Jesuits, 7-Day Adventists, 3-Day Eventists and Christian Fundamentalists, and I'd give most provincial estate agents a pretty wide berth as well.

However, things are never quite as simple as that. For a start, you may decide to leave some organisations well alone, only to find that they then come looking for you. I'm thinking here of some of the world's larger intelligence agencies, such as the CIA and the KGB. Frankly, rather than engaging them in common battle, which would be pointless and self-destructive, you would be much better off saving your energies and, instead, tackling them by some backdoor method that they would never expect. The Abercorns have found a way of infiltrating these agencies, using Jeff Jnr and his brilliant computer-in-a-pushchair, the Pramstrad. So let's tackle this straight away.

Practical Exercise: Infiltrating the CIA

Codename: Project Michael

There is no way we can predict where the threat will come from, or who will step in to try and scupper your efforts to rule the world, but even so and just for the sake of argument, why don't we suppose that, after a while, the CIA begin to find your amateurish efforts at World Domination rather tiresome, and decide to put a stop to your plans once and for all.

What should you do about it?

Well, to put it simply, you will need to hack into the CIA's central computer in the United States and cancel any orders that their agents may have been given to terminate your operations.

Q: *But isn't this dangerous, not to say illegal? Surely, if the CIA find you've been tampering with their computer, they'll send round four burly men in navy blue polo neck sweaters armed with baseball bats to put you right on a few things! I mean, it could get a little hairy, couldn't it?*

No.

Or, to put it another way: yes.

Well, perhaps . . .

Q: *Great, thanks. You've certainly put my mind at ease on that issue.*

Good. So welcome to Project Michael.

Project Michael: Phase One

Tell us what we're going to need, little Jeff!

'*Okay. The first thing you'll need is Lots of Expensive Stuff*'

Don't worry about the jargon. This is just high-powered computer-programming language for 'buying the right equipment'.

An ordinary portable cell-phone is essential – one that operates off the Cellnet system – as well as a lap-top computer, preferably a Pramstrad or, failing that, a Toshiba T3100-20 will do. Plus an *RS 2322C modem interface cable* and a *Terminal Emulation Program*.

If you know a thing or two about computers, you'll understand exactly what these are. If you know nothing at all about computers, then . . . well, tough! – you still need them, so ask your local computer stockist to explain it to you.

In short, though, everything must be small and portable so that it can be operated anywhere, thereby reducing your chances of being traced and caught.

'*Another thing you must have: the CIA's telephone number*'

In particular, their *modem phone number* so that your computer can dial theirs.

There are several recognised ways of obtaining this. For a start, you could always try guessing it, by dialling thousands of seven-digit telephone numbers at random in the hope of hitting upon the right one by chance – an idea which manages to be both brilliantly inspired and imbecilically stupid at the same time, if you don't mind me saying so.

It could take forever.

Indeed, the odds against your coming across somebody's telephone number accidentally are . . . well, put it this way: if you were to multiply ten by 1,000, then by a further 25,000, double it, subtract five, multiply it by the length of time (in minutes) it takes to get served in a British post office, then divide that by the goal aggregate of Aston Villa during the 1982–3 season; add the mean rainfall figure for Bolivia and the sum total of failed attempts made by Kathy Kirby to revive her singing career; multiply all of this by how many fingers I'm holding up right now, and you get some idea of what you're up against. Not an easy task by any means.

What is more, even if you do hit upon the right number using this method – and if you do, it will probably be sometime during the lives of your great-great-great-grandchildren – then the moment you dial it and try to log into the CIA's database, you will find yourself faced with another obstacle: something called Defender.

Defender, quite simply, is a protection device built into most major computers, which stands watch over the system day and night, like the ogre guarding the bridge in the fairy tale, insisting that none shall pass unless they tap in the correct password. This prevents interfering bloody-minded busybodies like us breaking into the database and screwing up twenty years of records and file-data at the touch of a button.

To gain entry, therefore, you must also find the key word or phrase that will unlock the electronic door to the computer's memory.

'So lastly, Item Number 3: you're going to need a password'
Correct. But there isn't just one password, there are hundreds of them.

Every agent has his own password to let him into the system: a special code which allows him, and him alone, to access the memory: a number, word or phrase that only he would know and which is easy for him to remember – the

99

name of his faithful old dog when he was a kid, perhaps, or his wife's maiden name, that sort of thing . . .

The purpose of Project Michael, then, is to discover these two pieces of information: the modem number and the correct password.

Project Michael: Phase Two
FINDING THE MODEM PHONE NUMBER
The telephone code for Langley, Virginia, where the CIA is based, is, if you're dialling from Britain, 010 1 703. In order to find the remaining seven digits that make up the modem phone number, Jeff Jnr goes about writing his own software program, one which, when fed into the Pramstrad, will try every conceivable combination of seven-digit numbers there is, jumbling them up and rearranging them over and over again until it comes up with the correct one for the CIA.

As you might imagine, this could take a little while.

So, meanwhile, to fill in time, the Abercorns set about tackling the equally tricky problem of finding the code-word.

The simplest way around this is to get your hands on a list of all CIA employees currently in service with the organisation. Do this by ringing their personnel office in Langley (010 1 703 482 1100) and asking them to fax a copy to you at once. I'm sure they will be only too happy to oblige. Stress the urgency of the matter and insist that you will use the information only for upstanding, proper and democratic purposes and nothing else. If for any reason they say no – which is unlikely, let's face it – then don't be downhearted. All is not lost, because by way of a short-cut and to help get you started, I am going to give you a top secret list of ten CIA agents presently operating out of the Langley HQ, together with their home-addresses, telephone numbers, names of faithful old dogs when they were kids and so on. All you have to do is contact any one of them and then somehow coax the information you need out of him.

Of course, there is very little the CIA would not do to prevent you finding out who their agents are; no steps they wouldn't take, no lengths they wouldn't go to, to keep this information from you. But threats alone are not enough to put us off. If we're going to take over the world, you and I, we must be fearless. Agreed?

Great. So here we go with the list. Be sure to make careful note.

SHORTLIST OF CURRENT CIA OPERATIVES

James Phil

Now, isn't that useful? Such a timesaver too!

But if anything happens – you lose this book maybe, or the CIA get to it first – then there is another way, Plan B. Though to do it, you will have to pack off one of your top agents to the USA as soon as possible, with an instruction to find and intercept one of their top agents.

Eager for frontline action, and despite her husband's profound misgivings, Julie has volunteered herself for this assignment. And so, next day, after tearful goodbyes all round, she wraps herself in a Boeing 747 heading Stateside, and makes her way to the state of Virginia.

Project Michael: Phase Three

Step One: Finding a CIA Agent   Langley itself is a pretty town. Less of a town, in fact, more of a suburb of the CIA building.

On the corner of Crozier Street and Rock Island Avenue stands a discreet cafe-restaurant called The Sheridan Diner, a popular haunt for CIA people on their lunch break from work. You should have no trouble spotting one – he'll be the chap in the corner, reading a copy of the *Christian Science Monitor* and muttering into the top of his pen.

Julie picks a guy at random: according to the security tag, this is Ted J. Kowalski of the Signalling (Intelligence and Information) Division, a genuine senior CIA operative in the field of Int and Inf. (Incidentally, in case you're wondering, all US servicemen and public servants are called Kowalski. It is an essential qualification for the job. So if ever you come across one who isn't, he's an imposter. Report him.)

Step Two: Winning the Secret Agent's Confidence   Following some brief chit-chat, mostly about the early pop career of The Applejacks, Agent Kowalski and Julie find they have a lot in common. For a start, it turns out that Kowalski has been stationed in Africa for three years, and Julie, by sheer coincidence, has seen the video of *Raid on Entebbe* twice, so from this point on, there is no stopping them and they chat happily for hours.

Step Three: Reconciling newly-acquired data with information previously gathered through British security sources
The weary pair unwind gently over Martinis then take a long shower together, licking each other dry before retiring finally to the bedroom, where Agent Kowalski lashes Julie to the bedstead with his braces, ready to give her a thorough porking. At this point, he slips out of the room, only to return several nerve-racking minutes later with half a tub of peanut-butter and a donkey.

More than a little intrigued, Julie waits, panting excitedly. After all, sexual favours are the accepted currency of international relations, aren't they? And one should never underestimate the bargaining power of an insatiable libido. So she simply lies back, thinks of England, thinks of Jeff, forgets Jeff, thinks of England again, thinks of what this will look like in The Movie, and then just enjoys every euphoric second of it, as Agent Kowalski takes her to heights of ecstasy she has not experienced since she stood in the rain for two hours outside The Palladium and got Vince Hill's autograph on the sleeve of her sweat-shirt.

Step Four: Tying up loose ends It is probably during the post-hump cigarette period that your CIA agent will give away the required information. And sure enough, it is while Julie is picking the last nuggets of peanut butter out from in between Kowalski's toes that he lets slip with his secret codeword for the CIA computer: 'Rascal' – the name of his dog when he was a kid! Told you so.

Step Five: Transmitting the information back to base The next morning, the two of them kiss fondly, then resolve to go their separate ways, she promising to keep in touch, he promising to divorce his wife the next time Julie's in town.

And that is that.

Later the same morning, armed with all the details gathered from Kowalski, Julie makes her way to the nearest fax bureau and sends everything back to Jeff in Witchester ready for phase four of this already rather longwinded operation.

Agent Kowalski talks about his dog.

Project Michael: Phase Four

This final part of the assignment is absolutely crucial, but also somewhat technical and potentially rather boring, so I'll try and breeze through it quickly. If, for any reason, you're not in the mood, that's okay. Skip the section for now and return to it another time when you need the information. The rest of us will plough through it and we'll meet up with you again in a few minutes' time at the start of the next chapter. How does that sound?

Great.

'Logging into the CIA's central computer'

Oh, we've started! Okay, so once Kowalski's details have been faxed to Jeff Jnr by his mother, and once the Pramstrad has come up with the seven-figure modem number of the CIA, as in due course it does, he dials it.

To do the same and to complete Project Michael properly, you will need the various pieces of equipment we talked about earlier, wired up as follows, making doubly sure that you are standing at a safe distance from the nearest telephone cell-site, so that the call cannot be traced back to your portable phone. Jeff Jnr has positioned himself in a large open field ten miles outside Witchester, which is ideal.

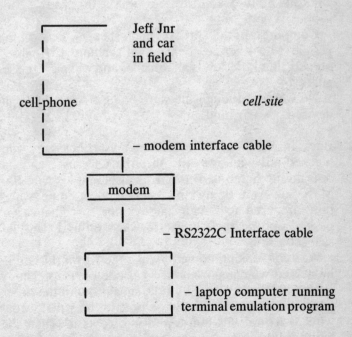

It won't be easy logging into the CIA's database, and I wouldn't want you to think otherwise. Computers like this one are a bitch!

To begin with, when you dial its number, the computer will immediately search for digital information at the telephone exchange to double-check the location you are calling from. So: i) If you use Kowalski's personal password but you're not calling from the address it knows to be his home, then alarms will go off and lights will flash in the security office at the Langley HQ to alert them of the unauthorised entry.

ii) On the other hand, if you *are* dialling from Kowalski's home, the computer will cut you off the moment you get through and call you right back on the number it knows to be Kowalski's. This procedure simply verifies that you are who you say you are. However, since you are not who you say you are – you're someone else entirely – then even a clinically brain-dead tortoise could see that you've got major problems here.

Computers of this sort are, in most cases, cleverer than the people who operate them, so it's bound to realise quite quickly that little Jeff is an intruder and will alert the security guards.

No worries, though, because being a smart little git, he's devised a way round.

Back in Virginia, Julie hires a mysterious grey van with blacked-out windows, the sort the CIA use, and parks it outside the home of Ted J. Kowalski and his wife Barbara-Mary-Sue-Ann. Being kinda regular down-home Americans, they are used to having anonymous surveillance vehicles parked outside their house for days on end, and so don't suspect a thing.

At a convenient moment, while the Kowalskis are heavily immersed watching a vintage episode of 'Roof-Tiles of the Rich and Famous' on TV, Julie sneaks out of the mysterious grey van, scales the telephone pole in the street, breaks the wire to Kowalski's house and intercepts it. Then she runs another line from the pole to her mysterious grey van, and from there connects it with Jeff Jnr's portable cell-phone outside Witchester.

Meanwhile, Jeff Jnr dials into the CIA computer, gives Kowalski's personal code word, 'Rascal', and the entry sequence starts to run.

Within seconds a menu appears on the screen: this tells Jeff Jnr firstly, what is for lunch today in the CIA canteen, and secondly, that he has an option of changing Kowalski's phone-number in the computer's memory to something else. This he does, making Kowalski's number the same as that of his own cell-phone in Witchester.

At this point, though, everything becomes ten times as urgent.

'Roof-Tiles of the Rich and Famous' won't last forever (it just seems to!). The moment it finishes and the real Ted Kowalski tries to log into the computer himself, giving the correct password and his home-phone number, he will be cut off and an alarm will sound. Defender will know instantly that Jeff Jnr has been tampering with the phone-lines and, boy, will he be in trouble then!!

So as soon as he sees the menu, Jeff Jnr instructs his mother to sever the line to Kowalski's house. This she does, after which it takes but a few hours for her to deliver the van back to the rental company, Mysterious Grey Surveillance Vehicles Inc., and return home to England and the Badger's Rectum, where she is greeted with heaps of praise for a job well done, a glass of Jeff's finest caterpillar wine, and what else but a lovely slice of Mrs Greenhalgh's white-hot dangleberry pie!

With this new-found freedom to roam around the database of the CIA computer as they please, the Abercorns are able to keep constant track of what all US government agents are up to. That means they can track down any orders the agents may have been given to scupper Jeff and Julie's world domination plans, and promptly countermand them.

But that's not all you can do with this procedure.

Back in late 1988, long before hacking was made illegal,

Jeff Jnr managed to open an untraceable numbered savings account at a well-known Austrian bank, ready for the secret deposit of huge amounts of church funds; he also sneaked into the *Reader's Digest* computer and removed his Dad's name from their monthly Lucky Draw read-out, and lastly, ordered the British Ordnance Survey computer to wipe all signs of Witchester from every map of England, making the town as untraceable as Jeff's bank account, if not untraceabler.

And that marks the end of Project Michael.

Doubtless you are feeling pretty damned pleased with yourself by now, aren't you? Of course you are! After all, what you've done here is quite something – far more than anyone else has ever done, that's for sure. And so you may feel like hanging over the hedge for a while and boasting to your neighbours about how successful you've been. Well don't, that's my advice. This is no time to rest on your laurels. There is too much left to do. You've got democratic governments to destabilise, dictators to unseat, coups to organise, satellite TV stations to set up . . . So no dawdling, right? Let's press on.

Besides, it's about time we joined up with those readers who were bored stiff by the computer hacking details and drifted off to wait for us in the next chapter.

Practical Exercise: Breaking Into a Top Secret Military Installation

Codename: Project Lynn

It is all very well having your own global religion with its lofty ideals and undercover terrorist cell, but I'm afraid that Terror Firma will never be taken seriously by any of our current world leaders, unless they also pose a substantial threat to the stability of world peace.

Sadly, that means you must join in the arms race. An unsavoury thought, I admit, but a necessary one.

No Superpower worth its SALT would dare hold its head up in the international community these days unless it had a whole arsenal of nuclear weapons to show off to its rivals. And since you intend to become a major political force too in the near future, it is obvious that you are going to need a bit of firepower of your own. Nothing overly ostentatious – a single atomic bomb large enough to flatten Paris or half of Canada should be sufficient. Because, as you will discover, world leaders are only ever prepared to negotiate with people who have the power to wipe them out.

However, the good news is that it's not necessary to possess the bomb itself in order to be considered a nuclear threat. Simply having the potential to build one is enough. And so the next stage in the Abercorns' World Domination Plan is to get their hands on a small quantity of plutonium-239, the isotope used to fuel nuclear reactors.

Project Lynn

Nature of Mission: To stage a night-raid on a top security nuclear missile store and procure eleven pounds of plutonium-239, or as much as will fit into two Sainsbury's carrier bags.

Location of Raid
The Curlies Nuclear Test Plant at Mastermaldon.

If you look at a map of Hampshire, you won't find Master-maldon shown anywhere on it. Not because it's a top secret munitions factory, although it most certainly is; nor because some of our most strategic atomic weapons research is conducted there, although it is. But simply because Master-maldon isn't in Hampshire at all, it's in Surrey – just north of the A4, in fact, between Thatcham and Newbury.

As sister-company to the larger Curlies Weapons Manufac-turing factory at Castleroy in Northern Ireland, the firm has been used by the government for over twenty years as a major source of experimental atomic research. Many of you, I'm sure, will remember the incident at Bikini Atoll in the South Pacific in 1954 as well as several underground nuclear tests on the Pacific islands of Ahu, Tavalu, Tofu and Uhuglu. In all cases, the initiative and the supply of bombs for these tests came from Mastermaldon. Indeed, some of our finest war-heads, missiles, rockets and explosives have been developed here, which is why, in recognition of all their hard work, the board of management at Curlies was recently given the 'Queen's Award for Bringing Armageddon That Bit Closer'.

Right now, they are working on another instrument of injudicious annihilation; something a little special this time and code-named The Beast, which is so hush-hush that not even the Russians know about it yet, although an insider from the factory recently described it as 'a fuckin' great rocket-type-thing that we're going to point at Libya'.

Anyway, regular six-monthly shipments of plutonium are lorried into Curlies to maintain a reasonable level of stocks, making it the perfect target for a surprise raid. The plant is gigantic, surrounded by two large fences – one of them electrified – and protected by sophisticated infra-red beams and guard dogs. Still, no building or base is completely impenetrable, so Jeff decides to send a team of crack insurgents into the area to have a shot at it.

Now, just in case there are some readers who have never broken into a top secret defence installation before, I'll just run through the personnel and equipment you will need and the procedure to be followed. It's quite simple, so don't worry. After all, if Matt Helm can do it, and he's only a fictional character, then I'm sure you can!

Personnel required

Uh-oh! And Jeff has a giant-sized problem right away.

This is a big job, indeed too big for Julie and himself to see through alone. The key to success in a mission of this complexity and danger can be summed up in one word: Teamwork.

And Trust.

Three words rather. But what can Jeff do? Both of his Crack Lesbian Insurgence Teams are either in training for their next mission, or else tied up in building the tunnel from Sea View to The Badger's Rectum. Clearly, he is going to have to resort to Plan B and make up a special team just for this mission. Which is why, not so long ago, he got into a top-level huddle with Julie and Mrs Greenhalgh and, after much thought, they came up with a fabulous plan: to make a charity pop video!

Q: *Make a charity pop video?? You're bloody joking.*

Nope!

By producing a soppy saccharine pop record and also a video to go with it in aid of charity, the Abercorns will be able to rope in a host of top showbiz names to support their cause, the way everybody else does.

Many major rock and film stars put a lot of time and effort into projects that raise money for such things as famine relief, although if each of them were to donate just a tiny fraction of his or her own personal wealth, they could probably rid the Third World of drought, disease, hunger and suffering until well into the next century.

The charity video idea is bound to attract acres of press and TV coverage for Faitheism. This, in turn, will help recruit followers, both young and gullible alike, from right around the country. Plus, and this is a big plus if you can pull it off, many of the famous people in the video may well be converted to Faitheism as a result of meeting you, and could

111

stay on afterwards to help you in your work. If so, these celebrities will be used to make up a special unit of soldiers assembled solely to stage the raid on Curlies Nuclear Research Plant.

Ingenious. So Julie quickly sets up her own charity.

However, as you well know, practically every disease, blight and disaster known to man has a separate charity begging for cash on its behalf, which means that new and deserving causes tend to be a little thin on the ground right now. Therefore, and in an act of mild desperation, Julie declares this to be . . . *Junior Baldness Week*. She then alerts the media to the fact that a pop video is to be made in aid of the Shave the Children Fund, and mails off invitations to every showbiz celebrity she can think of, and a few others she can't, urging them to give their time for free and take part. Those invited fall into three categories:

a) Top-Class Celebrity do-gooders

There really is no telling at this stage exactly who will be amongst the big-hearted few to put in an appearance, but by my reckoning Bruce Springsteen could be game for a song or eight, and you may as well count Phil Collins in too. Oh, and stick Jagger down as a possible, plus Sting, Freddie Mercury, Bonio of U2, and maybe even Paul McCartney – making one of those 'rare appearances' he seems to make so often these days.

These are your top-notch people-pleasers. They get top-billing on the sleeve of the record and are allowed to stand next to the camera when you're making the video.

Behind them there will be room for a few extra 'faces' to pad out the crowd, so it would be worth pitching for as many others as you can think of – say, Oprah Winfrey, Placido Domingo, Esther and Abi Ofarim, at least three members of New Kids On the Block, Jack Nicklaus, Stevie Wonder, The Beverley Sisters – Joy, Babs and the little sickly-looking one; Labi Siffre, Simon Rattle, Keith Moon, Martha Reeves and the Vandellas, Peter Ustinov, The Pet Shop Boys, Tammy Fay Bakker, and what's left of the Monkees.

NB. A quick warning here: it's a good idea on these occasions to issue everyone with a security pass to ensure that only the right people are allowed in.

I say this, not to keep fans and groupies away, but because there's a chance that a few personalities you don't want on the video might turn up as well. In this category, I'd put the likes of Bernard Cribbens, Bonnie Langford, Eddie 'The Eagle' Edwards, 'Diddy' David Hamilton, Ted '3–2–1' Rogers, Ed 'Stewpot' Stewart, Roy 'Bloody Irritating' Castle, The Krankies, Anneka Rice, Kenny Lynch and any other celebrity no-nos you can think of. I'm not saying they will definitely turn up unannounced, but they might. In which case, show them the door immediately or, if they slip through the security net, just make sure they stand right at the back somewhere, well away from the camera.

b) Political/social conscience types

We're talking in the region of your Glenda Jacksons here, and your Susannah Yorks, and possibly your Annie Lennoxes and Jimmy Somervilles as well. And a Kenneth Branagh or two wouldn't go amiss either if you have them to hand, although chances are, to goad figures of this calibre into the arena you'll probably have to be fighting for a truly major cause – some monumental injustice, such as prisoners in South America who need freeing pronto, something worthwhile like that.

What I'm really saying is that Junior Baldness in itself may not be exciting or innovative enough to get their militant juices flowing.

The best solution, therefore, is to try doing a trade with them and see if they nibble at the bait. Try promising that, when you do take over the world as planned, then you will grant an instant reprieve for the African elephant and any other creature on Schedule 2 of the Endangered Species list. (A somewhat empty promise, as it happens, since the African tusk-collection business is worth a whacking 170m quid a year at current prices, and could be harnessed to put money into your own coffers. So think on: don't act too hastily on this one.)

In addition, offer a faithful pledge to sort out longstanding conflicts in Palestine, Iraq, the Lebanon, South America, Northern Ireland and wherever else, and to step up the fight

113

on rain forest destruction; tell them you'll bring back the birch and free all prisoners of conscience the world over; and also guarantee that, from now on, vegetables and fruit will be wholly irregular sizes, riddled with worms, scarred by insects and for the most part rotten and inedible. That should win you the support of the anti-insecticide lobby, and may just – again, who can tell? – *may* just be enough to tempt Meryl Streep to fly in especially for the session. Although, on the down side, Pamela Stephenson and Rula Lenska could become curious and show up as well, which is the last thing you'd want. So be careful.

And lastly, c) *Complete Nobodies*

It is always a good idea at times like these to swell the cast of your video with a sprinkling of faces which people really ought to recognise but don't: has-beens, famous these days principally for appearing on crap charity records like this one. They'll turn up for almost anything that gets their profile on-camera in the desperate hope that it might revive their horribly flagging career.

This lot have enjoyed their fifteen minutes of fame already, and have been packed off to Has-Been Heaven where they now languish eternally, waiting for walk-on parts in TV soap operas or a guest appearance on the back row of 'Blankety Blank'.

Every now and then, their luck changes and someone flings them a rope ladder of hope – a comeback tour maybe, or even a walk-on part in 'Knots Landing', and all of a sudden they emerge, blinking, into the limelight once more, basking in this new-found public recognition, before becoming so giddy in the slipstream of unscheduled popularity, that they topple right back down the hole again. Catch them before they do and include them in your video. And don't worry if they're all out of tune or can't sing a note – after all, many actors are like that. Simply record the song anyway and call it Deaf Aid. You'll make a fortune.

Once the video is all wrapped up and the mass of actors and vocalists have drifted away, some to make charity records elsewhere, others to collect their dole money, you should be left with a few celebrities who have been won over by the cause you are fighting for and who will now wish to support you in your struggle. Of course, if you couldn't predict who would turn up for the video in the first place, you are definitely not going to know who will be left over afterwards. So everything from now on has to be guesswork.

From our notional crowd of do-gooders, therefore, just let's say that The Pet Shop Boys have stayed on, as has Stevie Wonder, Ted '3–2–1' Rogers, Martha Reeves and the Vandellas, Oprah Winfrey, The Krankies and Peter Ustinov.

It's not a lot to go on, I know, but if you leave behind Ted Rogers and The Krankies – and I do sincerely urge you to – then with a couple of weeks' hard training under the robust but lovable supervision of your West Country housekeeper, the rest of the group may well forget that they are just pampered variety performers and will no doubt, in time, gel into a powerful and co-ordinated fighting unit – physically fit, aggressive, thinking as one, and ready for the mission.

This, then, is your Celebrity Undercover Nuclear Team (see over).

On second thoughts, scrap The Pet Shop Boys!

Keep the team small – stick to Oprah, Stevie, Martha, the Vandellas and that lovable old rogue Peter Ustinov.

Plus, if there is room on the minibus, you may as well take a few Twilighters with you, just in case any personal sacrifices have to be made along the way. This is an insurance policy more than anything else, since in any tight spot, old soldiers like these can be depended upon to summon up the Dunkirk spirit and put on a spunky display of fake martyrdom, keeping the enemy at bay whilst shrieking, 'Leave me, leave me – I am old. You've got your whole life ahead of you. Run!' In these circumstances, don't argue with them, just get the hell out of there.

Four geriatrics should be enough, I think, and these will go to make up your Senior Citizens Reserve Operations Team for Undercover Missions.

Three tips, though: firstly, be sure to brief your pensioners

Out on manoeuvres with The Pet Shop Boys.

in full before you set off; secondly, keep them warm and busy. Why not give them a complicated jigsaw to do on the bus? One with lots of sky in it, that should do the trick; and thirdly, promise them a peaked cap and a medal if they survive the mission, or an engraved marble headstone on a hillside overlooking Arnhem if they don't. They'll love that.

Finally, in the Abercorn camp, as a last-minute confidence-booster for herself and her troops, Mrs Greenhalgh picks up a copy of *The Witchester Echo*, and reads what kind of forecast Kosmik Kirsty is making for her starsign. On the day of the raid, her predictions are clear:

> **Libra** With Mercury in retrograde until the end of the month, you should put off signing contracts or finalising important deals 'til then. Affairs of the heart are well-starred, and Wednesday could mark a turning point in one special relationship, so say it with flowers and just watch the result! This is also a great time for night-time assaults on top secret defence stations.

Uncanny!

Equipment needed for the raid

117

You must take *all* of the following items with you, otherwise you needn't bother setting off:

a) A pair of large industrial wire-cutters;
b) A thermos flask full of crushed ice;
c) A duffle-bag containing several large block magnets, as powerful as you can make them;
d) A standard aluminium A-frame;
e) A can of Mr Sheen furniture polish;
f) A chainsaw from your local branch of Homebase;
g) A pair of rubber kitchen gloves or, better still, some heavy-duty insulated industrial gloves;
h) David Jensen (the dog, not the immensely popular radio and TV celebrity). He should be carried in a bag with the other equipment until needed. Don't worry about whether you are being unnecessarily cruel in this situation. After all, it's only a dog!;
i) A long, strong rod and some insulation tape;
j) Several pairs of cotton gloves and booties;
k) Two members of The Minipops dance troupe.[7]

THE PLAN IN OPERATION, AT LAST!

Okay, then, taking it step by step, let's quickly run through the various stages of the raid, from the Team's arrival outside the perimeter fence of the base at 2 a.m., to their safe return to the Badger's Rectum with the plutonium two hours later.[2]

1.40 a.m. Minibus turns off the A4 trunk road near Mastermaldon and pulls up in the dense wooded area to the north-east of Curlies Defence Installation.

[7] An eighties singing and dancing sensation. The Minipops were a group of precocious child performers, each of whom seemed to have set his or her heart on being the next Bonnie Langford, without first checking whether there was, in fact, any demand for another one. At a volume of several thousand decibels, they entertained theatre audiences everywhere with their successful blend of leaping about in bright costumes and yelling pop songs at the top of their voices. If they ever re-form, fight to get a ticket.
[2] These points and many more are set out in greater detail in an incredibly useful Board of Transport pamphlet called 'Missile-Bases and How to Infiltrate Them', written by Benkt Eekhof-Stork, author of that other indispensable do-it-yourself anarchy manual, 'Stage That Coup!'

118

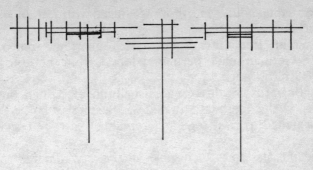

Aerial view of Installation.

Unit sits in silence with the lights off for twenty minutes.

Or, if silence is asking too much, then games may be played, such as 'I-Spy' and 'Whose Groin Is It Anyway?' Or alternatively, members of the team could try working out what 'minibus' is Latin for. Or 'Bisto' even; e.g. Bisto: 'I make rich, brown gravy without lumps in it from a packet'; Bistas: 'You make rich, brown gravy without lumps in it from a packet'; Bistat: 'He or she makes rich, brown gravy . . .' and so on. A fascinating game which really helps pass the time, depending on how good you are at conjugating convenience foodstuffs.

2.00 a.m. Oprah Winfrey disembarks and, whilst the others check their equipment, she unties the two Minipops from the roof-rack.

A word of caution here: Minipops are often fresh out of stage-school, so, for the time being at least, it is best to keep them securely gagged with their hands bound behind their back. This will deter them from launching into a spontaneous medley from 'Joseph and The Amazing Technicolor Dreamcoat'.

The Senior Citizens Reserve Operations Team for Undercover Missions can be left on the bus doing the jigsaw until they are needed. Mrs Greenhalgh, Oprah, Martha Reeves, the Vandellas and Peter Ustinov all proceed to the fence, leaving Stevie Wonder to keep look-out, a task to which he is singularly unsuited; but burglars can't be choosers, as Mrs Greenhalgh often says.

119

From this point on, they are faced with three major obstacles.

2.06 a.m. Encounter first obstacle: outer fence, one of the tough, German-made perimeter fences from the notorious 'Big Bastard' range.

Big Bastards like this one are usually not electrified, but are at least twelve feet high, topped with a spiral of barbed wire and watched over at regular intervals by infra-red security cameras.

The initial step is to disable all security cameras within a fifty yard radius by attaching to the underside of each one a large block magnet. This will cause the picture to scramble on the monitor in the guard-house, effectively knocking out the camera. Alas, it may also alert the guards to the fact that something is wrong, so you'll have to get your skates on.

Q: *Excuse me. May I just check something with you before we continue?*

By all means.

Q: *This is all totally illegal, isn't it? Not to say incredibly dangerous. And if we go through with it, we are not only committing criminal damage to private property but also indulging in theft of the most serious kind, plus treason, terrorism and breaches of our national defences, all of which are punishable by hefty fines and extremely long periods of imprisonment.*

That's right, yes.

Q: *Oh my God!*

2.09 a.m. One of the Vandellas chainsaws *quietly* through the wire of the fence, creating a hole big enough for everyone to climb through.

We now have what is known, in missile-base infiltration circles, as a 'beyond the perimeter fence situation' – a bit of jargon you needn't concern yourself with. In essence, it means you're now beyond the perimeter fence and ready for obstacle number two.

2.16 a.m. Encounter next obstacle: a set of four low-powered infra-red laser beams nailed to a post. You should be able to find the post, but you won't see the beams since each one is no thicker than a chipolata and only half as visible. Cross them inadvertently, and you will set off a mass of security alarms in the guard-house.

How the hell do you get through them, then?

This calls for a can of Mr Sheen furniture polish.

Oprah takes the can and sprays it lightly into the air in front of her. As millions of tiny droplets of furniture polish fall to the ground, they glisten in the path of the infra-red beams and show everybody where they are. At this point, the two Minipops can be slung roughly across to the other side, whilst a couple of the Vandellas erect the A-frame over the beams. Everybody crosses the frame one at a time.

2.21 a.m. Third obstacle: a second fence – one of the very latest German-made fences, of the 'Even Bigger Bastard' variety.

This one is fifteen feet high and *is* electrified. At 200 volts, the current is not strong enough to kill anyone, but it could severely barbecue you if you touched it with your bare hands. Imagine sticking your tongue into a light socket – it's like that.

So rubber-gloves on!

Another big hole needs to be cut through this fence, using the heavy-duty industrial wire-cutters which Peter Ustinov has in his bag, and remember, because of the current, no part of the piece you are removing from the fence must touch the ground until the entire section has been cut out, otherwise it will be in contact with the earth and the alarm will sound.

2.34 a.m. Did I say three major obstacles? In that case, add a fourth: pressure-plates.

Once through the Even Bigger Bastard you must still exercise caution because the area five or six feet beyond it may be booby-trapped with electronic plates buried an inch or so underground and which activate an alarm if you tread on

121

them, or it may even be landmined to outwit more persistent intruders. So it makes sense to bring some kind of proper mine-detecting equipment with you.[8] However, failing that, a bit of on-the-spot make-do ingenuity should see you through . . .

. . . which is, I'm sad to say, how the Abercorns lost their latest pet David Jensen, a cute animal and a loving one too, of whom they were growing very fond. Still, 'another day another dog', as Julie often says – and anyway he died in the cause of global enlightenment which must count for something when the RSPCA decide to prosecute.

2.49 a.m. Once through the fences and the mines, their way is clear straight through to the nuclear reactor silo, which is housed in a squat, unimpressive building covered with corrugated tin and is well-lit and clearly signposted as 'Radiation Pulse Facility', making it easier for rebel insurgents to find it in the dark. Other surrounding buildings, labelled 'Nuclear Effects Laboratory' and 'Vulnerability Test Centre', merely show they are on the right track. Otherwise, they are of little interest.

And here is where our Undercover Team encounters the trickiest part of the entire mission. Their success depends largely on whether the guards at the base (and there are as many as forty soldiers in what is called a Special Reaction Team), and more particularly the one patrolling outside the reactor silo, are long-standing fans of Martha Reeves and the Vandellas.

Time is short, and therefore it helps if we suppose for the moment that they are, by sheer fluke, lifelong Vandellaphiles.

That being so, Martha Reeves steps out of the darkness and begins to run through her repertoire of sixties hits, from 'Dancing In the Streets' to 'Honey Chile', whilst Oprah

[8] Anteater Clearmine Co. Ltd in Dalglish, Scotland, supply professional mine-detection and clearance equipment at reasonable rates, I'm told. If this is true, then why not give them a call and ask if they have anything suitable for breaking into top secret military bases? I'm sure they must have a brochure.

Winfrey and Mrs Greenhalgh keep watch and Peter Ustinov, actor, director, writer, humorist and renowned after-dinner speaker, nips inside the building.[9]

2.56 a.m. The interior of the plutonium store is guarded by what is known as PIR – a passive infra-red alarm, primed to detect any movement in the room. So Peter Ustinov takes a handful of crushed ice out of the thermos flask and puts it on top of the alarm sensor, a little black box with a tiny winking light on it in one corner of the room. The cold from the ice serves to de-activate the sensor inside the alarm.

Next, the great wit and raconteur ambles over to the control room to fetch the two keys which unlock the padlocks on the door of the reactor. Once unlocked, the door will slide open and the reactor can be raised up from its steel-walled pit underneath, by flicking the white switch inside.

Lastly, Ustinov, dressed in cotton gloves and booties, lifts two pieces of plutonium out of the reactor and drops them into his specially-prepared twelve-inch-thick, lead-lined Sainsbury's carrier-bags, filled with dry ice.[10] He then lowers the remaining isotopes back into the pit, slides the door to, locks the locks, returns the keys to where he found them in the control room and leaves.

3.01 a.m. Meanwhile, outside, Martha is winding up her fabulous sixties' medley and the guard is beginning to get itchy and suspicious.

---

[9] I am assuming here that the door to the plant has been carelessly left ajar, otherwise that spells big trouble for our courageous team. The outer door to the reactor building is made of steel ten inches thick and takes three keys to unlock it. The key to the middle lock is in the possession of one of the guards in the Special Reaction Team; the others are held separately by two physicists with authorised access to the reactor. And so, to save the narrative from becoming even longer than it already is, I'm assuming the door's open. Okay? Good.

[10] Two separate pieces are necessary. One is a plutonium sphere about the size of a baseball, with a deep hole in it, and the other is a plutonium cylinder which fits flush into the hole in the ball. The two must be stored in separate carrier-bags so that they do not make contact and destroy half the country.

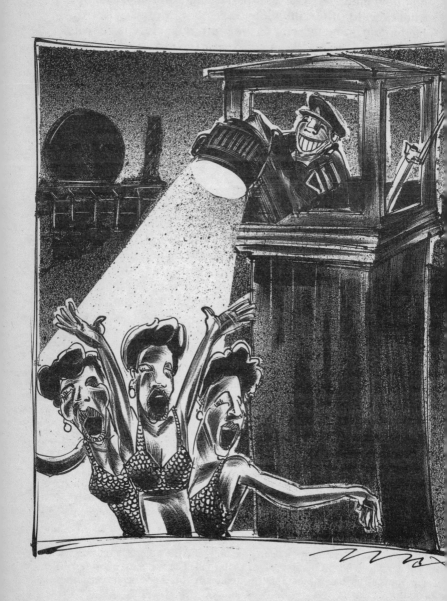

So, to keep him distracted, and to fill in time until Peter Ustinov emerges with the plutonium, Oprah steps in to interview Martha about her career at Motown Records, beginning in the early sixties as a secretary in their A&R department, right up to when she left the label in 1972. Martha talks frankly about her alleged bust-ups with Berry Gordy and Diana Ross during that time, reveals the story behind one of her biggest hits, 'Jimmy Mack', and also tells of the part she played in the Austro-Hungarian Uprising.[11]

3.03 a.m. Ustinov emerges from the reactor silo with the carrier-bags and drags them through the hole in the Even Bigger Bastard, over the A-frame, under the perimeter fence and away towards the minibus, as Oprah winds up the interview by springing a last-minute surprise on Martha: out from behind the reactor silo come Diana Ross, Lionel Richie and girls from the original line-up of the Vandellas when they first formed way back in the early Motown days. In tears, Martha embraces them all warmly and then ends her set with a couple of R&B riffs from her heyday, together with a bluesy cover version of 'Ernie – the Fastest Milkman in the West'.

3.27 a.m. Well into the second encore of 'Honey Chile', and quite suddenly, several armed members of the Special Reaction Team come running from behind a far building with tracker dogs.

3.28 a.m. Surrounded by guards and desperate not to be captured lest they screw up the chance of an upcoming two-week stint in Vegas, the Vandellas untie the Minipops and throw them at the dogs, whilst the one-time Queen of Motown and her backing vocalists, together with Lionel Richie, Diana Ross, Mrs Greenhalgh and Oprah make a speedy escape through the fence. Oh, and don't worry about the Minipops, incidentally. Sure, they could well be savaged to death by the crazed alsatians, but try not to be too sentimental about it. Think of it more as a mercy-killing. Let's face it, if they had lived, they might have had their wish and grown up to be just like Bonnie Langford – by comparison to

---

[11] Which I happen to know is nil, so it's going to be a very short interview!

which, a slow grizzly death at the jaws of a dozen hungry guard-dogs somehow seems quite attractive.

3.30 a.m. Back to the minibus, ready for a thirty-minute drive to the Badger's Rectum, stopping only twice to let members of the Senior Citizens Reserve Operations Team for Undercover Missions nip out for a piss. Otherwise, mission successfully completed, exactly as planned and on time.

One last word. Plutonium must always be handled with respect and great caution. It should be stored securely in dry ice, inside containers lined with lead. When carrying the ball and cylinder, they must not be joined together, since this is what causes them to react, and they should not be touched with your bare hands – either wear cotton gloves, or, preferably, use a pair of tongs.

And there you have it. Project Lynn is obviously a resounding success, and once the Celebrity Undercover Nuclear Team is back at the Badger's Rectum, Julie hands out mugs of hot Benfica to everyone as well as mouth-watering slices of dangleberry pie, whilst Jeff uncorks a bottle of his best Edam claret and Lucette alerts the media.

First thing she does is telephone Billy 'Hey-Hey-Super' Divine at Witch FM, and also a solitary journo manning the overnight newsdesk at *The Witchester Echo*, claiming responsibility for the theft of the plutonium. She tells them that Terror Firma were behind the raid, that the nuclear bomb they plan to make as a result will be used for peaceful purposes only, and that the world will be hearing from them again soon. That should put the wind up The Men In Grey Suits!

Once word leaks out that two bags of plutonium have been pilfered in a daring nocturnal raid on the Mastermaldon Nuclear Research Installation, Terror Firma are sure to be regarded in all international circles as a force to be reckoned with; a move which will amplify the Abercorns' effect on world affairs and enable them to move on quickly to the next stage of the Plan.

The seeds you have sown over these tricky few weeks must now be nurtured lovingly whilst they are left to stand in the

Use a pair of tongs.

warm compost of confusion for a little while. Money will continue to pour in from Healthruherbs and The Most Unholy Church of St Thomas the Doubter. The religion, together with its various sinister activities, should attract huge amounts of comment, publicity, money and followers, with several spirited individuals setting up their own sub-branch of St Thomas' in their own area.

Time, therefore, to leave well alone here, to look beyond these shores and teach a few foreigners a thing or two. That calls for a new chapter, though, and a bright new heading as well.

But first . . .

Special Envoy Update

The latest news just in from Beirut: as predicted, Archbishop Abercorn's special envoy to the Lebanon, Mr Carmichael, the tramp from the Precinct, got rat-arsed in the hotel bar during an eve-of-mission knees-up, and began thrashing members of Hezbollah (The Party of God) randomly about the face and neck with a Black and Decker Strimmer.

As a result, and quite rightly, he has been taken hostage and locked up in a basement somewhere to the west of the city.

From this point on, Mr Carmichael can be written off as their overseas operative. He's a gonner, they'll never get him back. Pleas for his safe return, negotiations with impartial go-betweens, press conferences, top-level diplomatic man-oeuvres – all are a total waste of time and energy. Indeed, they may only result in his release, which would be disastrous. So why bother?

Simpler by far just to appoint a new envoy.

This time it's the turn of Duggie's longtime friend and co-alcoholic, Vince 'Donkey-Dick' Osmond, whose grubby demeanour, together with his profligate use of the F-word in general conversation, make him the ideal successor to Mr Carmichael and a dead cert in talks with religious leaders the world over.

However, to keep the press at bay, Jeff sets up a sham support group called The Friends of Duggie Carmichael, under the aegis of Donkey-Dick himself, to monitor ongoing developments in the Lebanon, appear in numerous TV documentaries and news programmes on the subject, and also to organise a reunion each year on the anniversary of Mr Carmichael's abduction, in the half-hearted hope that his captors will somehow relent and set him free. However, since this is doubtful, all members of the support group plan to sit patiently by the telephone for a little while – maybe even as long as twenty minutes – and if nothing is heard by then, will bugger off down the pub to get legless in his memory!

OPERATION DOTRICE:
Overseas Initiatives

You don't have to be especially brilliant to realise that global power can never be achieved unless, at some point, you reach out overseas and spread the word of Faitheism to distant lands. The Healthruherbs business, too, needs to become international if you are to win the hearts, minds and wallets of ordinary citizens everywhere.

Broadly speaking, for our purposes, there are three sorts of countries in the world today: those we will have to bargain with (China, for instance, which is too big and too highly populated for us simply to waltz in there and conquer it); those we can invade ('banana republics', 'bilberry colonies', 'seedless tangerine sovereignties', etc); and those you have to overthrow gradually using the democratic process itself. The countries in Western Europe, and increasingly Eastern Europe, fall into this last category, and it is these we must attend to now.

Practical Exercise:
Overthrowing a Western Democracy

Codename: Project Roy

Let's start with Europe, then. Which country shall we pick on?

As a general rule, try and choose a country that nobody likes and which is despised by all its neighbours. Choose a country where the people are arrogant, stubborn, suspicious, hostile, selfish and lazy, whose administration practically strangles itself each year with its petty-mindedness and snail's-pace bureaucracy, and whose bastard government is largely responsible for screwing up global weather patterns thanks to their persistent nuclear testing in the South Pacific. Choose a country where your activities are unlikely to be discovered – one that is not overpopulated, simply because nobody in their right mind would ever live there by choice.

That should narrow it down a little for you.

Still not sure?

Well, here to help you, is a list of countries which fit the bill exactly, and which would make an excellent site for your European operations. Those countries, listed in alphabetical order, are as follows:

i) France.

Oh. Whereabouts in France?

Somewhere remote and unremarkable is best. I suggest Amiens, a smallish, flattish, boringish town situated roughly ten miles west of Montelimar, *comme la corneille vol*.

Amiens only has one feature worth mentioning and you'll find it towards the centre at Place Alphonse Fiquet. It's an apartment building called La Tour Perret, which, by some unseemly whim of the architect who designed it, has been fashioned into the shape of a giant brick penis twenty-seven

131

storeys high, and which now dominates the entire Amiens skyline – not because it's especially attractive, but simply because once you spot a dick *that* big, it's very hard to take your eyes off it!

As for the rest of the place, you will find it a grim, charmless wasteland, uninhabitable except by the French, and for that reason if no other, it would make a superb hideaway for your base of operations.

Anything more you can tell us about it, besides the size of its penis?

Sure.

Basically, Amiens is a town for timewasters, where the locals fritter away half their life sitting outside countless pavement cafes in all weathers, drinking cappuccinos that taste like Daz Liquid and smoking themselves half to death.

Indeed, smoking is not merely an accepted habit hereabouts, it's a must – a social imperative, and as much a part of the ordinary French way of life as laziness, bad driving and being rude to tourists. Heavy smokers are the elite in this town. There are several fashionable bars and clubs in Amiens where a rasping cough is considered the height of chic among teenagers, and if you don't chain-smoke by the age of ten you're practically an outcast. Which explains why, by mid-afternoon, dozens of bistros throughout the town are flooded with schoolchildren playing catch-as-catch-cancer, committing slow ciggy-suicide in a desperate attempt to be considered one of the crowd. Indeed, 40% of babies in French working class homes are weaned off their mother's milk and straight onto tobacco, by way of preparation for an active social life in years to come.[1]

What's more, you'll find the same pattern repeated throughout Europe: alcohol and tobacco fulfil an urgent need in empty lives; they help pass the time and bond whole sections of society together. Remember, we learned this earlier: people don't like to be left out of things. They would rather risk suffering heart disease, cirrhosis of the liver,

[1] Figures courtesy of Concoctastat Ltd.

132

premature ageing and a dozen other similar nasties, than be considered a freak or an outsider different to everyone else. Therefore, if your friends smoke, you smoke. They drink heavily, you drink heavily. They do drugs, so do you. That's how most people are – sheep! Which is great for us, because it means the battle is half-won already.

The Frenchies are appallingly weak-minded, so if it were to be announced one day, quite unexpectedly, that the world's Gauloise resources were running out and cigarettes were about to be rationed, the entire French social network would be devastated. There would be nothing left to live for, or to die of; except maybe alcohol – and if tobacco and alcohol together were so heavily taxed that it took them out of the price-range of all but the wealthiest of men, there would be a peasants' revolt within weeks, and possibly even a full-scale civil uprising.

The French take killing themselves very seriously indeed.

Sorry, I don't get you. Where is this leading?

Okay, then. Your first task is to set up a branch of Terror Firma in Amiens, okay? After which, *their* first task will be to nobble various members of the French parliament, as well as key individuals from opposition parties, using techniques explained in Chapter 2.

Nobble the politicians one at a time and then, after injecting them hypodermically with a large dose of everybody's favourite intravenous barbiturate, Hypnoven, prime each one hypnotically with a single major idea: that they must go back to the French parliament and support a motion that taxes on tobacco and alcohol should be raised to such a ludicrously high level that absolutely nobody in the country will be able to afford to buy them. (If you are looking for an excuse for this deprivation, try claiming that, hypothetically, you are doing it for the sake of good health, conservation and clean air. It may be a load of old bollocks, but it sounds good, and in the world of politics that's all that matters.)

Given sufficient time – a month or two at the outside – the idea will eventually percolate through to the statute book and then to every home in France via the media, fuelling an immediate civil uprising.

Such as mass demonstrations, you mean?

That's right. From this point on, the anarchy machine more or less switches to automatic: a black market quickly develops in drink and tobacco, billions of francs are lost to the French economy in excise duty, the government's competence is challenged openly; widespread outbreaks of civil disobedience continue with demonstrations a hundred-thousand strong, clashes with riot police, sit-ins and mass arrests.

The French students will be out in force, of course, as they usually are at times like this. In most colleges, studying takes a very low priority when there's the chance of a good punch-up to be had. They will march through the streets of Amiens, in their brightly-coloured polo-necks and duffel-coats, past the statue of Mireille Matthieu, coming together in the shadow of the giant brick prick to taunt the town councillors with wicked jibes of '*Vous avez des visages comme des morses*' ('You have a face like a walrus'), and '*Je veux heurter ma balalaika contre vos reins!!*' ('I'd like nothing better than to smash my balalaika into your kidneys' – this loses much of its venom in translation, but you get the idea anyway.)

Of course, buses will be overturned en route and set alight (buses are always overturned and set alight in riots, it's a tradition), onion-sellers will be tipped off their bikes and have their berets stamped on repeatedly (not a tradition as yet, alas, but it ought to be). Before you know it, tabloid newspaper offices are being burned to the ground, all driving test examiners have been rounded up and pelted with ballbearings, and packs of restless youths are prowling the streets, chanting the lyrics to 'Chirpy Chirpy Cheep Cheep', as they burst into newsagents' shops and insist on reading magazines without paying for them and then march on local government buildings, demanding instant reforms and an end to delays and red-tape, with cries of:

> 'What do we want?'
> 'An end to procrastination!'
> 'When do we want it?'
> 'How about next year?'
> 'Oh, all right, then.'

And lastly, in a final demonstration of working-class solidarity, student leaders will invade Charles de Gaulle airport outside Paris, and fling themselves into the engines of Boeing 747s as they taxi down the runway. The French are nothing if not extreme.

Chaos, anarchy, social and moral disintegration, destabilisation of the System . . . Hurrah!

What you have here is a revolution in the making. But you mustn't fool yourself into believing that protest alone changes anything. In sufficient numbers it may do: look at Czechoslovakia, look at Romania, look at Tiannenman Square (on second thoughts, don't look at Tiannenman Square!). But more often than not, out of a crowd of 200,000 protestors, only ten people are there to do any protesting, another thirty or so have turned up because they've never kicked a policeman in the face before, and the other 199,960 are probably members of the press.

A NATION IN REVOLT

Now imagine this same procedure being repeated in dozens of other democracies right around the world: ideas implanted by hypnosis into the minds of government ministers so that they vote to deprive the general public of their favourite pastimes and addictions.

A stroke of genius.

For instance, you could try banning football matches in Brazil, a country whose people live, breathe, talk, sleep and even play soccer. You could bring about massive tax increases on alcohol in Australia ('The Bevvy Levy'). Or why not increase the price of contraceptives in America? By introducing a Sin Tax, you will effectively ban safe sex for ordinary people. Hell, is *this* going to put their backs up?? And if you want to annoy them even further, try giving your idea a fancy

135

name – 'The New Celibacy' perhaps – and support it with a few doddering bespectacled experts in white coats saying that regular sex is the prime cause of leukaemia and that abstinence is good for you. That should go down well.

Also, you could use your influence over the government to introduce a 'Clean-up TV' campaign which is so thorough that it wipes practically everything off the schedules; everything, that is, except Baptist hymn programmes, weather forecasts and cookery shows for the deaf. Or why not bring the public transport network to a virtual standstill by withdrawing government subsidies to the railways and bus companies? Impose a 9 p.m. curfew seven days a week for everybody under forty-five years of age; give generous tax concessions to the very rich and withdraw all allowances to the elderly and infirm. It's endless: you could have so much fun.

And if the hypnotic thoughts have been planted properly in the minds of the elected representatives in each country, they will be unable to reverse their decisions, yet equally unable to work out why they shouldn't. So that, as the government's political credibility slowly crumbles, you and your Terror Firma Party will emerge as the nearest credible alternative to the present system in any future election.

In your manifesto, you promise to reform the current rules and pledge to restore things to how they were before the changes – abolish Sin Tax and the Bevvy Levy, bring back regular rumpy-pumpy, reduce the duty on ciggies and lager. Be seen as the party which plans to put things right, the one that is going to return the status quo, that will press the short-sleeved shirts of oppression on the ironing-board of democratic policy-making, as Mrs Greenhalgh might say.

You'll be in power before you know it.

Are people that stupid, though? Will they fall for this?

Of course. No doubt at all. They are sheep, they're not like us. What one does, they all do.

Sheep adore the status quo, they prefer things to stay the way they always were in the past. Because the past is over, it is safe and does not hold any fear for them. That is why people always treasure the golden shadows of yesteryear, and why they seem to reminisce constantly about the Olden Days, when summers seemed longer and warmer and it always snowed at Christmas time; when TV sitcoms were funnier, pop records had tunes you could hum and Michael Jackson was still only a damp patch in his father's lap.

Those were the days, eh? When policemen solved crimes and missing children were always returned home unharmed; rivers were unpolluted, homosexuality hadn't been invented, and Daz soap powder wasn't speckled with all those horrible little blue bits like it is now. Wars were important then too, and worth fighting for, and you could eat all the fat you liked, including half a pound of lard three times a day for twenty-five years, and your arteries would never clog up.

Everything was better all round, wasn't it, in the Olden days?

Well, the short answer to that is no.

The long answer is 'no it wasn't'.

Things were actually worse in the past, often much worse, but because the future is so uncertain and because people live in fear of the unknown, they long instead for what they mistakenly believe were better times in a bygone era. Which means that, when you and Terror Firma come along, as the party whose manifesto promises to bring back those mythical good times and put everything back the way it was, then frankly, a referendum will be almost academic. You'll win any election hands-down, leaving everybody wondering how the hell you managed it.

Q: *You make it all sound so straightforward. But the people who run the world at the moment, whoever they may be, will surely not take kindly to us intruding on their patch like this. And what about people such as the Iranians or Libyans, or big underworld organisations like the Mafia — won't they be just a little bit cross with us?*

Hmm, you may have a point.

THE MAFIA
When it cmes to dealing with the Mafia and their likes, I

imagine you are, once again, out of your depth and you should therefore leave well alone – that is, if you know what's good for you. Although, even if you *don't* know what's good for you, but suspect that living a little longer and keeping your knee-caps might be, you would be as well to take my advice seriously: don't mess with the Maff!

'Compromise, make allowances, and ensure that you survive to the end of the book,' that's Jeff's motto.

In addition, there is no telling who is a member of these organisations and who isn't. Anybody could have connections with them, anybody at all. For instance, journalists have been trying for years to establish some kind of link between the Mafia and legendary crooner Frank Sinatra. Now, these rumours may or may not be true, there's no way for us to know; but either way, it makes the point – you can never tell who has Mafia connections and who hasn't, so doo-bee doo-bee dooooh-be careful. Don't tamper with these people, don't ask too many questions, and you'll be okay.

Having said that, though, Jeff is keen to persuade many of the more notorious underworld families to clean up their act, put aside any differences they may have, lay down their weapons and agree to a series of arms-reduction talks with his new special envoy, Vince 'Donkey-Dick' Osmond. There's no guarantee of success, of course, and they may take great exception to his suggestions, but it's worth a try.

Finding the Maff

To meet up with the Mafia, you could travel to Southern Italy and then ask the first person you meet to tell you where members of the Maff hang out. According to the brochures, practically everybody in Italy knows a member of the Mafia, because practically everybody in Italy *is* a member of the Mafia. However, failing that, if you're a bit strapped for cash and a trip to Palermo is out of the question, then all is not lost. There is somewhere else you could try.

Queensway, Bayswater, is a broad concrete wind-tunnel in London, along which are blown representatives of every nationality in the world at some time or another. At No. 345 Queensway, is a large, airy patisserie called 'The Royalty', where thick-set middle-aged Italians, each with beautifully-coiffured hair and a Rolex the size of a half-brick, arrive at regular intervals in chauffeur-driven six-wheel stretch Mercedes with blacked-out windows and a satellite dish on the roof, trying not to be conspicuous. After a quick glance each way, they dive straight into the cafe, many on crutches after a particularly boisterous game of 'Trivial Pursuit' the previous evening led to several broken hips and a couple of random manslaughters.

Like The Badger's Rectum, The Royalty serves as a front for the London operations of many gangland heavies.

There are various tell-tale signs inside. Customers are huddled around tables in threes and fours, sipping coffee and chatting excitedly, as they unfold detailed building-plans of The Bank of England. Others sit back, barking instructions into a Vodafone and absent-mindedly polishing their rifles. Nobody speaks English, least of all the waitresses, so think on: if you want to negotiate with anyone in The Royalty, don't forget to buy a phrase-book and learn a bit of the lingo. Nothing too fancy, just a few key Italian words and phrases which may come in useful when handling the Mafia:

a) *Vi ho portato i soldi, adesso mi restituite i miei nipoti?*

I've brought you the money, now may I have my grand-children back?

b) *Questa roba è veramente cocaina o soltanto farina?*

Is this really cocaine or just self-raising flour?

c) *Ho trovato questa nel mio letto, credo che sia la tua.*

(Whilst holding Shergar's head) I found this in my bed, I think it must belong to you.

d) *Dio Cristo, ha una pistola!*

Christ Almighty, he's got a gun!

e) *Credo di essermi sporcato i pantaloni*

I believe I've soiled my trousers.

f) *Guardate il codice dove le cifre corrispondono alle parole, poi continuate alla nota in calce, lo scoglierete?*

Excuse me, I appear to have been shot fourteen times in the head and chest. Is there a doctor nearby?

g) *Buongiorno Badessa, e che bella mattinata, non è vero? Comunque, venendo alpunto: ci sta inseguendo una banda di assassini spietati. Come vede, sono stato ferito gravemente, forse anche fatalemente, ed il mio amico qui ha bisogno di mutande pulite eduna trasfusione del sangue. Quindi, potremmo approfittare della sua gentilezza per cibo, alloggio e un posto sicuro finché non sia passato il pericolo?*

Top of the morning to you, Mother Abbess, and what a fine morning it is, to be sure. Actually, I'll get to the point: we are being pursued by a gang of ruthless hitmen. As you can see, I have been seriously wounded, perhaps fatally, and my friend here needs clean underwear and a blood transfusion. Might we therefore impose upon you for food, shelter and a safe haven until such time as the danger is passed?

h) *Ma come no? Ha aiutato Julie Andrews, puttana!*

What d'you mean *no*? You bloody helped Julie Andrews, you bitch!

These guys will not compromise; they will expect you to speak their language, and so if the only Italian you know is 'Is this the way to the station?' then I'm afraid you're not going to get very far. Well, as far as the station perhaps, but no further.

In short, treat them with respect. Remember, there are finer people than yourself propping up motorway bridges all over the West Midlands. So promise not to tread on their toes or intrude on their patch, and you may escape with your genitalia hanging where you left them.

DEALING WITH LIBYA AND IRAN
Tricky.

Some countries in the world today are a law unto themselves and, as hard as this may be to imagine, will have no wish to co-operate with your plans to overthrow them. Iran is one example. Their attitude has been typified in recent years by the venomous ramblings of Ayatollah Khomeini.

Things you should NOT say to the Ayatollah Khomeini
Everything from 'Hello' onwards basically. He's dead.

Things you should NOT say to Colonel Gadaffi

Ditto. He's not dead, but you'd probably be wasting your time.

Gadaffi is seen by his enemies as a Libyan[2] terrorist who should be wiped off the face of the earth a.s.a.p. Alas, whoever designed and built the planet realised this and organised things in such an unfortunate way as to ensure that those whom the Superpowers class as lunatic dictators would be sitting on the world's largest supplies of high-grade oil, making any strategic nuclear assault economically impossible.

These countries are therefore free to behave as badly as they like in the global arena with little chance of retaliation, which is why they usually emerge from every diplomatic scuffle with little more than a few bruises and a good ticking off from the United Nations.

But Gadaffi, like all dictators, has a flaw. He is a well-renowned egotist, and by far the best way for Jeff and Julie to coax him into backing Terror Firma is by cheap flattery. To that end, then, every member of the Abercorn family has had his or her hair permed as a gesture of goodwill prior to their trip to Tripoli.

Also, if international gossip is to be believed, Gadaffi would be prepared to provide money and weapons to any movement whose purpose was to undermine and cripple a Western capitalist democracy. All he'd want in return would be sophisticated radar technology, combat training for his armed forces, and Julie's recipe for hotpot. A small price to pay in the circumstances.

---

[2] Incidentally, for readers with a lesser grasp of world affairs, this is his nationality and not his starsign.

Q: *But what happens if the police suddenly get wind of our links with the Mafia or Colonel Gadaffia, and declare us to be 'wanted men'? Or what if they send in the army? Won't that set our cause back a bit?*

What a little worry-wort you are, to be sure!
Tell him, Jeff.

Jeff says . . .

'Like the police, all members of the armed forces are subjected, over years of training, to intense conditioning which pounds away at their resistance and drums into their minds that they must obey orders without question.

'It is a form of very intense hypnotism, compelling them to subjugate themselves to the good of the team, follow any commands they are given and even risk their lives out of an automatic sense of duty and comradeship. And because they are hypnotised in this way, any command, however extreme, provided it is given by a recognised superior officer and preceded by the words, "You are ordered to . . ." will switch them immediately into Obedience Mode, and from then on they will do exactly as they are told to do. They have no choice. If they don't agree with the orders, they must leave the service, they dare not disobey them.

'Your best solution is once again to follow the nobbling instructions we gave earlier. Find the top man in the army, the navy, the air force and the police, shoot each one up with a dose of Hypnoven, and plant into their subconscious minds that they will follow any orders you give them without question.'

143

Q: *And finally, before we move on, you mentioned China, a country in which our plans are unlikely to go down a storm, I should think. And Russia too. I mean, if they'll slaughter their own people for trying to bring about radical change, what would they do to us?*

A highly intelligent and stimulating question, if I may say so, and one I would like to return to in due course. Do you mind?

Q: *Well, no, I suppose not. You won't forget, though, will you? This is important.*

I won't forget, I give you my word.

Q: *Righto, then.*

Fine. Because, having overthrown a few Western democracies by now, you will have a lot more confidence in yourself and your World Domination Plan, and will want to begin toppling a dictatorship or two as well. Unfortunately, the rules are slightly different here, not quite as straightforward, and the best way of learning how to do it, is to do it.

So, just as an exercise, let's take a country at random and invade it. Some place in South America would be okay, or maybe even Africa. Somewhere with an undemocratic regime that nobody has ever heard of.

Hey, I say! How about Cameroon?

Q: *Where?*

Perfect.

Practical Exercise: Let's Invade Cameroon![3]

Codename: Project Karen

THE REPUBLIC OF CAMEROON – SUMMARY

a) Where is it?
Africa.

See?

b) Oh, right. Anything else you can tell us about it?
Sure.

La République Uni de Cameroun, as it's called in French, is the second richest of the Central African States and the fifth largest cocoa exporter in the world. This alone is a good reason for invading it. You would only have to slap an embargo on all cocoa exports, and a third of the world's population wouldn't be able to get to sleep at night.

You see? – you've got to think 'clever' all the time.

---

[3] For the benefit of readers who take our advice and actually go so far as to carry out this attack, and to help maintain the vital element of surprise, Hodder & Stoughton have kindly agreed that *The World Domination Handbook* will not be published in the Republic of Cameroon in the foreseeable future, which is nice of them.

145

In the western part of the country lie broad fertile plains covered in rich vegetation, where herds of canteloupe a thousand-strong roam freely, migrating throughout the year between here and the foothills of the Tchabal Mbabo to the North East. And it is across these same plains that packs of wild denim can be found, just waiting to be rounded up, slaughtered and turned into jackets. To the south, you'll find lush coastal pastures punctuated by magnificent equatorial forests and slow, majestic rivers – the sort of scenery that keeps Kodak in business.

And in case you were thinking that the rainforests might prove to be too much of an obstacle when you are hiking through them on foot, don't worry – like other forests around the world, these too are being sawn down bit by bit every year apparently without being fully replenished; so with any luck they should have been cleared completely by the time you get there.

Weather conditions differ from region to region, although, being close to the Equator, Cameroon tends to be quite warm all year round. In the capital, Yaounde, summer temperatures can reach as high as hot-and-stuffy centigrade (that's stifling-and-unbearable fahrenheit), and rainfall has been known to be as much as forty feet per annum in some areas, so remember to take a mac![4]

Cameroon's population of 9.6 million is split into tribes and scattered thinly throughout its ten provinces, although this crude total of 9.6m includes thousands of refugees who have fled here from persecution under the existing regime in neighbouring Chad. Between them the natives speak around 300 languages, the favourites being English, French and Ewondo. Welsh is not spoken anywhere, as far as I know; or if it is, it's only done in private between consenting adults. Much the same as in Wales really.

Politically, Cameroon operates very successfully along the

---

[4] If you don't have a proper raincoat, that's okay, just buy one when you get there. They are available all over the country and will be on sale in any streetmarkets you happen to visit. Just ask for a Cameroon Mackintosh and they'll know what you mean.

lines of a benign dictatorship – a highly prosperous one too, thanks to its booming economy. Since becoming a republic sometime between 1922 and 1968, there have been two presidents, although traditionally in regions like this – where a nation's leader often arrives in a coup and leaves in a coffin – the identity of the guy in charge usually depends on who gets up in a morning and feels like doing the job.

The majority of the population are far removed from their government and care little about its workings. In most cases, as elsewhere in Africa, survival alone is the purpose of their empty lives. And anyway, let's face it, with more than 300 languages to learn, they don't have time to bother about who's running the bloody country, do they?

On the whole, this is a mysterious, beautiful place, full of wonder, tradition and warm, inviting people just sitting there waiting to be conquered. Of course, once you have imposed your will on them and brought the population to heel, life won't be quite as wonderful, beautiful and mysterious for them as it is now. But even so, the persecution of dissidents is so severe under regimes in neighbouring countries that it makes widespread oppression by a foreign dictator seem quite attractive really.

So why waste any more time? Let's invade Cameroon!

e) Hang on. If I do decide to give this invasion idea a go, will I not be opposed by the powers of the media in Cameroon?

Certainly not.

The grip of the media is nowhere near as strong in Cameroon as it is here. TV and radio stations are few, as are newspapers, although what papers there are were snapped up years ago by Media Moves International Inc., the global communications conglomerate headed by Sir Nigel Barkham-Twist (still pronounced Bassett). His Cameroonian portfolio now includes such noted journals as the *Sambolabbo Evening Chronicle*, the *Fundong Herald* and *The Wum and We Observer* (incorporating *The Nkambe Gazette*), all of which will be on your side, simply because Sir Nigel himself is on your side.

147

f) Incidentally, sorry to break in again, but what happened to points c) and d)?

Oh yes . . . I apologise.

c) Any permits or jabs needed?

Before you can really get down to the business of overthrowing the government in Cameroon, you'll need to go there. And before you can do that, you will need a visa. Either apply for one before you set off, or alternatively you can ask for a ten-day visa when you arrive (ten days should be quite long enough to show the buggers who's boss!).

Incidentally, on the visa-application form, where it says 'Purpose of visit', you'd better write 'holiday'. Don't put 'to subjugate the masses', or 'overthrowing government'. And in the space marked 'your occupation', write anything you like provided it's an ordinary job. Don't put 'Messiah' or 'Spiritual Father to Millions' or any one of a dozen other titles that might fuel their curiosity and give the game away.

Also, two weeks before you go, you should be vaccinated against yellow fever, cholera and one other deadly disease, the name of which I forget for the moment, so check with your doctor.

d) Can I drink the water?

Yes you can, but typhoid is nowhere near as much fun as it's made out to be, so I should avoid drinking it wherever possible.

g) What's the best way of getting to Cameroon?
Malaria!!

h) Really? Is that their national airline?
No, malaria is the third major disease you need to be vaccinated against before you set off. I just remembered.

As for getting to Cameroon, and since you want your invasion to come as a bit of a surprise, the question you have to ask is: should you send your lesbian task-forces altogether in one group and risk being asked awkward questions by the authorities, or should you divide them into two separate units and dispatch them at intervals?

Well, Jeff found himself with precisely this dykotomy. The answer, though, was simple: split them into two Crack Lesbian Insurgence Teams, just like before. Ten women per team: either 'bleached blondes versus bottle brunettes', or 'persons of sound parentage versus complete bastards', or even 'those who find Benny Hill amusing, versus those who think he's a slimy voyeuristic old git whose sexist infantile gags are not only painful to watch but they're also an insult to the intelligence of right-thinking people generally', etc etc.

Once divided up like this, C.L.I.T. 1 should then fly to Douala, Cameroon's principal port and business capital, which is situated on the Mouthfulofbenylin Peninsula in the Gulf of Guinea. At the same time, C.L.I.T. 2 should be making their way by road from neighbouring Nigeria towards Cameroon's administrative capital Yaounde, and thereafter onto Douala where they will rendezvous with C.L.I.T. 1.

Maps of the area can be obtained from the Topographical Institute, 36 rue Joffre, Douala, Cameroon. A word of warning here, though. On an ordinary map the distance from Douala to Yaounde looks to be about this far: I————I, but when you actually get there, you'll find it's about 1,000 bloody miles! So be careful.

For the unit assigned to travelling overland and encountering border guards en route, it may be enough to allay their suspicions if you tell them that you're embarking on a fortnight's backpacking tour of the Cameroonic hinterland, taking in Kumba, Bamenda, Mundemba, the crazed-albino-dwarf encampments around the base of Mount Awol, and the scenic wonders of the Tchabal Gangdaba.

But Jeff has had a better idea altogether.

He has arranged for his second unit to pose as a small-time theatre co-operative, touring with their own stylised production of *The Emancipation of the Doughnut-Makers* by

149

Gluck,[5] around many of the smaller towns and villages in the foothills of the Tchabal Mbabo – places such as Makalele, Mba and Wogomdou, before moving down to Kumbo, Ndu, Sonkalong, Wannti, Wum, We and Njini Kom, and finally onto a twelve-night stint at the Douala Hippodrome.

A show like this affords you the perfect opportunity to meet up with thousands of ordinary Cameroonian people and convert them to Faitheism. During the interval, the ushers could hand out free copies of The Abercorn Authorised version of the Bible, fully updated and revised, leaving out all the extraneous bits from the original which Jeff thinks are irrelevant: i.e. most of the Old Testament and all references to God and Jesus in the New Testament, and including instead dozens of useful phone numbers, some first aid information, a range of quick-snack recipes for busy Mums and page after page of handy household tips in a series of cut-out-and-keep gift cards. Another merchandising hit!

i) I've got bad feet. Do I have to walk the whole 1,000 miles?
Not necessarily.

For their overland trek, the Abercorns have hired a lorry and have also bought a small number of second-hand Czechoslovakian cars as a job-lot from a dealer in Southend who understandably wishes not to be named.

Assuming you do the same, then your group of Skodas (actually, I'm not sure what the collective noun for them is, although 'an eyesore of Skodas' seems appropriate), will be used as transport throughout the invasion, and therefore should be very heavily armour-plated. Three cars ought to be

---

[5] *Not* one of Gluck's best, to tell you the truth, but if anyone at the border tries to test your alibi by asking for a summary of the plot of the show, just say that it's a simple tale of two nymphomaniac seamstresses, Nina and Tutte, who leave their home in turn-of-the-century Gdansk to look for adventure arounds the tavernas of backstreet Leningrad in the early 1950s. Songs from the show, such as 'The Gynaecologist's Lament' and 'A Fool and His Toupee . . .' have since become classics in Poland, although exactly why that is remains a mystery.

enough in all: one for diplomatic missions, and a further two which can be used whenever the situation calls for a show of military might.

j) It all sounds terribly complicated. Would it not be a good idea to enlist the help of some local agents in Africa, just to oil the wheels of the revolution a bit?

Good thinking, and the Abercorns have found just such a person – he's Jimohola-Aiwiola, their little sponsored African child over in Ethiopia. Jimi speaks fluent Ewondo and will organise transport for the lesbian groundtroops, as well as laying on false permits, detailed plans of the Presidential Palace and signed photographs of Winnie Mandela for anybody who wants one. Let's meet him.

KEY PERSONNEL PROFILE 7: JIMOHOLA-AIWIOLA ABERCORN, ETHIOPIAN AGENT

The Abercorns adopted Jimi several months before this book went into print, in a shameful gesture of black tokenism and as a way of dodging any accusations of racism that might be levelled at them. Jeff thinks it's a cracking idea. Indeed, he often says that if he had five pounds for every Ethiopian child he has adopted over the years, he'd have . . . well, five pounds actually. Jimohola-Aiwiola is the first.

The eldest of twenty-nine children, Jimi lives in a tumble-down mud shack in a village 200 miles north of Addis Ababa. He is very religious and firmly believes in life after death – in fact he firmly believes he's experiencing it right now. If he grows up, his ambition is to have twenty-nine children of his own and give them all the things he never had – such as adequate food and shelter, and maybe even a regular bus-service into Addis Ababa. However, though they may be poor, everyone in the family survives as best they can, farming the land and harvesting the crops for sale around the village. Jimi even makes a few extra pennies each year by posing for overseas charity posters.

The Abercorns regard him as as a key element in their world domination efforts, which is why they have entrusted him with looking after 'the Ethiopian end of things'. Of course, it involves very little just yet, so instead he concerns himself with taking care of his brothers and sisters, at least two-thirds of whom are sick and dying. His constant requests to the authorities for money for food, better housing and warm clothing as well as funds to help build irrigation channels in the parched fields around their home have always fallen on deaf ears, although he did strike lucky recently when he asked the Ethiopian government for a sixty million pound grant to build a nuclear-missile launch-pad nearby, complete with rockets aimed directly at neighbouring Eritrea, and received the cash within two days.

k) *And finally, what is the best plan to adopt when overthrow-ing a benign dictatorship?*

Hmmm. Well, in the case of Cameroon, your first task is probably to locate the Presidential Palace, which is at 37 rue Etienne Daho in Yaounde, and find out the name of the guy who happens to be running the country on the day you get there. Then manoeuvre yourself somehow to within anaesthetising distance of him.

You could storm the palace, that's one option open to you. If so, be warned: parking nearby is very restricted, so remember to fix a 'Disabled' sticker to the windscreen of your diplomatic Skoda while you're inside. Ensure too that everyone in the team limps severely for the rest of the mission.

Again, when staging an invasion, you should go armed with some key phrases appropriate to the situation in one of the country's native tongues, such as Ewondo. Something like 'Hands up, this is a siege' and 'I've got a potato-peeler, so no funny business or the guy in the crown gets it,' should be enough.

An alternative to storming the palace, however, is to wait until the president ventures outside to attend a function of some sort, and nab him then.

Being head of state means turning up at an endless round of glitzy balls and other important occasions. So for example, one night he may be hosting a banquet in honour of the third ex-wife of the Secretary to the Assistant Deputy Subpostmaster-General of the Philippines; whilst on the next, he will be special guest at the opening of a new donkey sanctuary or the Central African premiere of Andrew Lloyd Webber's latest smash hit, *Wincey!*, a musical charting the career of former game-show hostess Wincey Willis, from her humble beginnings as a TV weathergirl and wildlife-lover, to her lesser role as adjudicator on a television treasure hunt game called, not inappropriately, 'Treasure Hunt', and thereafter her passage into Has-been Heaven when it was suddenly and inexplicably axed.

Wherever you happen to nab the Pres., shoot him up at once with a dose of Hypnoven, and then programme his thoughts so that, from this moment on, he will: i) agree to implement every policy that is handed down to him from Terror Firma HQ in Witchester;

ii) actively promote amongst his people the religion of Faitheism, setting up churches for non-believers in every

153

major town and settlement throughout the nation and giving his personal endorsement in TV commercials to all Heal-thruherbs' products, with the catchy tag-line, 'Buy this, or you'll be extradited to Chad!';

iii) sign a treaty consenting to Terror Firma becoming a major force in world politics.

And that's it! Just repeat the same process systematically in every other dictatorship throughout the world and you will soon be well on your way to total power. Sure, it may be a long and expensive haul, full of obstacles and setbacks, but a gratifying one all the same.

SPONSORSHIP

As I say, invading other countries can be a mighty expensive business, what with the cost of airline tickets and the excess-baggage charge for your weapons etc, so you may not wish to pay for the whole enterprise out of church funds. If that's the case, it might be worth considering a sponsorship deal of some kind.

Try contacting Richard Branson, for instance, and see how he feels about stumping up for the cost of the trip. He's got money, influence and plenty of aircraft; win him over, and he might just fly you to Africa and back for nothing. In return, you could undertake to stencil the word 'Virgin' on your luggage, uniforms and rifles and across the forehead of every lesbian you take with you.

Alternatively, you may be tempted to hi-jack an aircraft.

HI-JACKING

If a sudden violent death lying face-down on cold tarmac is the very next item on your Life Agenda, then I recommend you hi-jack an airliner as soon as possible. Otherwise, there is only one piece of advice I'd give you – don't do it! Hi-jacks are terrible things, quite self-defeating in every way. They almost always end up with somebody being shot, and nine times out of ten that somebody will be you. Either that or the plane has to be detonated as a defiant gesture to the authorities, killing everyone on board – yourself included.

In the meantime, you spend three days sitting in a DC-10 at

Cairo Airport, eating nothing but airline food (the usual menu: Check-in Risotto, Crème Carousel, Pilot-Error Mousse aux Fraises . . .), and surrounded by two dozen Egyptian police marksmen who can afford to hang around until the end of the century if needs be, while you decide whether to shoot the cabin crew and dump their lifeless bodies out of the starboard hatch onto the runway, or to fly the plane to Budapest singlehanded without an instruction manual.

No, life is much too short for such folly – don't do it! Pay for your flight if necessary, just make sure you stay alive.

6

Long Time No Siege

That's not really the name of this bit at all. Someone at the publishers thought it would make an hysterically funny name for a chapter. To be honest, I prefer the old title . . .

6

Time to Dupe the Electorate

That's more like it.

Now, it's one thing to go overthrowing some piddling little dictatorship on the other side of the world, but quite another to take control of a sophisticated parliamentary democracy like Great Britain and make it part of your empire. You can't just barge in and start telling millions of ordinary British people what to do and how to run their lives, because they simply won't stand for it.

Instead, a better idea is to sow the seeds of discontent amongst the general public by creating civil unrest of some kind, the way you did in France. You could try organising a National Anarchy Day, for instance.

Q: *Here we go again. Another crackpot scheme*

Not necessarily, you haven't heard it yet.

NATIONAL ANARCHY DAY

On National Anarchy Day, millions of your followers right across the country will be instructed to withdraw all their money from the high street banks, sell their stocks and shares, boycott major chain stores, supermarkets and boutiques, post no letters, resign from trades unions, abandon public transport, ignore all car-parking restrictions, pay no bills and take an impromptu day off work.

If it's a success, or even if it isn't, do it again a couple of days later. And again two days after that. Keep on with it, over and over again. The results could be amazing.

For a start, there'd be an immediate run on the major banks, which would only serve the pompous, arrogant, thieving gits right. Banks have had it all their own way for far too long. They only open when it suits them, they send their staff to lunch at the busiest times, leaving only one cashier to serve a queue that stretches halfway down the high street; and, worst of all, they take the money from *our* savings accounts and invest it all over the place, making colossal amounts of profit, which they then keep for themselves! It's a scandal, and they deserve all they get.

With a string of well co-ordinated Anarchy Days, billions of pounds would be lost to these big institutions. Elsewhere, trade would dry up, shops and factories would be forced to lay off staff and finally to close; the stock market would be driven to a state of near-collapse and big business would perish under the sheer weight of popular opinion – hurrah!

The end result? Support for the government of the day would wane, propelling the country into a general election – double hurrah! And that is when you whip out your trump card and turn Terror Firma from a mere worldwide religious phenomenon with a £100 million-a-year turnover, into a bright new political party.

This may be your one and only chance to put the world to rights, to tackle the crime rate, punish offenders in a manner which really teaches them a lesson, and to rid society of the major injustices which we, as citizens, know are wrong but which successive governments made up of weak-minded,

157

corrupt politicians and self-serving committees, repeatedly fail to do.

So don't screw up, all right?

Another point: when the time comes to call your party something, think back to all that stuff we said earlier about choosing a decent name. Make it strong, forward-looking, innovative and, if at all possible, completely meaningless.

I suggest 'The New Right'.

Okay, so it seems a bit feeble at first, but put it in bold type and just look what happens:

The New Right

See? Much better.

Chief among our proposals is a pledge that, once the New Right party is voted into power, we will give to every person in the country over the age of eighteen, *an immediate tax-free sum of £100,000*, which will be sent to them within two weeks of the government taking office. That's one hundred thousand smackers in their hand – guaranteed!

After all, everyone wants to be well-off, don't they? To be able to pay their bills promptly, buy that new car, take two holidays a year, send their kids to private school and college. And besides, no-one can resist a free hand-out. That's why this is such a scorcher of a plan, one which is bound to clinch a landslide victory for us, and all but demolish the opposition.

The rest of Jeff's policies are contained in a massive document running to over 700 A4 pages. It could have been completed in just 100 pages, but if he had done that, people might have read it and then he'd be in *real* trouble!

So here's a quick summary of the manifesto, which Jeff has christened, rather catchily I think, The Bene Diktat.

The Bene Diktat: A Summary

1) The home address and telephone number of all convicted burglars will be published regularly in at least three national daily newspapers, for the benefit of their victims or anyone else who feels that the courts don't do nearly enough to teach these bastards a lesson.

On top of this, all proven child abusers will have the words

'I molest small children' tattooed across their forehead in thick blue lettering; convicted rapists will no longer receive jail sentences – instead, they will be taken to a public place and have their testicles crushed between two breeze blocks, either by their victim or by someone who'd quite like to do it; and similarly, a terrorist found guilty of murder would be brought face to face with the bereaved family of his victim. Every member of the family would be given a baseball bat and left alone with him for up to two hours in a locked room, after which he would be taken away in a bucket and flushed down the toilet.

2) Personal taxation is to be made a matter of individual conscience.

3) All circuses will be abolished forthwith, and arrangements made for the animals to be confined, taunted and humiliated elsewhere.

Most people only visit the circus once in their life anyway, staying just long enough to find out how ghastly it is then leaving immediately, never to return. However, for a long time, travelling circuses served a very useful purpose, being the easiest, most convenient way for East European dissidents to defect to the West. They would masquerade as extremely tame trapeze artists, performing only with the aid of a net and a harness, and then only if the trapezes were no more than one foot six off the ground. After eight or nine performances at the most, they would usually pack their things and disappear, to set up home under a false name in a suburb of Brussels.

Nowadays, thanks to the diffusion of East–West tensions, they simply accept postings overseas as diplomats instead – that way they can defect *and* be paid for it!

4) A private bill will be introduced to make David Bowie get his teeth capped.

5) Something called a Citizens (Right of Retaliation) Act will be introduced, legalising physical assault on certain kinds of people within society who annoy certain other kinds of people within society.

In other words, rather than taking them through a lengthy, exorbitant and often unjust legal system, you can mete out the appropriate penalty yourself on the spot. Three sharp blows to the head or crotch will be the maximum: just enough to knock them to the floor and teach them a lesson. If the punches result in injury or accidental death, so be it: that was the risk they ran by doing whatever they were doing in the first place.

This right of retaliation may be exercised on any of the following:

> people who drop litter; dog-owners who allow their pets to defecate copiously on pavements, in gutters, or on other people's front lawns; unhelpful public officials; people who talk loudly in cafes and restaurants; Michael Winner (this is an exception to the standard three-blows rule: if this becomes law, you will be permitted to punch him as many times as it takes to knock that nauseating clown's grin off his smug little face!); salesgirls in department stores who jump out from behind display cabinets and spray Musk deodorant in your eyes as you walk past; Morris dancers; barbershop quartets; vomiting drunks who deposit large pools of what looks like Pot Noodle every four yards along the pavement on their way home from the pub; women conducting street surveys; people who've undergone open-heart surgery and who insist on showing you their scars over dinner; drug-pushers; vandals; traffic wardens; bye-election candidates who heckle you from the top of passing estate cars using a loud-hailer; late-night car-door slammers; greasy middle-class students who stand around shopping-precincts trying to sell copies of *Socialist Worker*, but only because they're too young to remember what an unruly monster true socialism really is; Australian backpackers; estate agents,[6] owners of car-alarms which go off regularly at two in the morning, waking up everybody within a fifty-yard radius – except the owner himself, of

---

[6] Another exception to the three-punch rule. The best way to punish an estate agent, in my experience, is to tie him securely to a chair, then take his mobile phone, dial the speaking clock in Rio de Janeiro, place the phone on a table across the room, and leave it.

course, who usually lives two streets away and can't hear it; theatre-goers whose electronic watches go peep-peep-peep every quarter of an hour during operas; people who never use underarm deodorant even on sticky, sweltering summer days; and finally, anyone found to be wearing a Nolan Sisters 1982 tour jacket who, when asked politely, refuses to take it off and set fire to it.

As a secondary part of this bill, there will be three extra provisions:

a) Firstly, no vaccine, drug, nerve-gas, toxin or chemical compound can be tested on any animal unless it has been tested on a leading scientist first;

b) Secondly, members of the public will be issued free of charge with a small steel mallet called a 'githammer', which is to be used whenever another motorist either blocks your driveway with his car, nicks your parking space or double-parks so close to you that you can't get your car out. In the absence of the culprit himself, thereby making the statutory three punches impossible, the frustrated victim will be permitted to use the mallet to smash the word 'GIT' into the bodywork of the offender's car, as a reminder to the selfish arrogant little scumbag that other people have rights too!

c) And finally, any major corporation found to be discharging huge amounts of effluent and toxic waste into our streams, rivers, lakes and oceans, will be brought to book by a special Anti-Pollution Court. Once the case is proven against them, each member of the board of directors will be made to drink four pints of water taken from around one of their waste-disposal pipes.

6) Christmas will no longer be a merchandising free-for-all lasting four or five months. Instead, the countdown to it will start officially on the first day of December, in order to turn it into a special occasion once more. Anyone caught celebrating Christmas before this date will be taken out and given a jolly good seeing-to by a platoon of armed military personnel.

Included under this head would be carol singers found on street corners in early August grovelling for loose change, and grasping store managers who hang 'Merry Christmas and a Happy New Year' signs in their shop as early as mid-September, in the hope of wringing every last drop of goodwill out of their customers before their competitors do.

7) Modernist architects who design outrageously obscene structures and so destroy the skyline of our most beautiful cities, are to be concussed with a house-brick, then bound and gagged, locked in a trunk and pushed off Beachy Head.

It is a common misconception that anyone who qualifies as an architect has, by virtue of that qualification, the wherewithal to design buildings. This is simply not so. Indeed, it is just one of a whole list of popular misconceptions that have filtered down through the ages unchallenged, and which still remain to haunt modern society. Others include:

i) if a guy is black and drives a Porsche, then he must have stolen it:

ii) doctors know how to cure things;

iii) the more famous a pop star is, the more talented he must be;

iv) the waxworks in Madame Tussaud's are breathtakingly lifelike;

v) apart from one or two bad apples, policemen are upstanding, honest, dependable and clean-living souls;

vi) building extra motorways eases traffic congestion;

vii) rainy days are bad days. (You can put this down to years of conditioning by the media. Just because a bit of adverse weather happens to inconvenience a few motorists, it doesn't mean that the rest of us can't enjoy ice, drizzle, blizzards and thick fog. We don't, as it happens, but we should be free to without being branded as loonies.)

8) It will be made a criminal offence for television companies to release classic comedy and drama series on video, induce their viewers to go out and buy them, and then repeat the whole sodding lot on TV a couple of months later, when they could have been taped for nothing.

9) MI5, MI6, the CIA, KGB, Special Branch and all other intelligence services operating secretly within this country, will be obliged to hold open days four times a year, so that the public can walk around and pry into *their* affairs for a change. If this proposal proves to be a success, then it will be extended

in due course to the Inland Revenue, police and armed forces, debt-collectors, credit card companies and census offices.

10) A referendum will be organised as soon as possible on the reintroduction of the death penalty and corporal punishment, as well as the need for Sunday trading and round-the-clock licensing hours. The public is forever demanding these measures, but they always seem to be blocked by a minority of vested business interests and stuffy old religious fanatics who are sixty years behind the times anyway, and who would bring back boy chimney sweeps and the ducking stool if they were given half a chance.

11) Officials at the Ministry of Defence will be forced to reveal at a well-publicised press conference that UFOs are a hoax, that aliens are not visiting earth and indeed never have been.

Information will then be put on public display, showing that so-called flying saucers are really only new military craft, currently still in the experimental stage. They work rather like those trains in Japan, the ones with linear-induction motors that use magnetic force to travel at phenomenal speeds. Defence boffins have been delighted over the years with the public's gullibility in this area and with the volume of wild space-ship propaganda that has been spread about. The more fake sightings there are, the more these distract people's minds from what is really happening – which is nothing whatsoever.

Action will also be taken to tell tourists that there is no such thing as the Loch Ness Monster – it is simply a recurring publicity stunt – and that 'haunted' olde-worlde pubs in Britain are indeed haunted, though not because the dead are still walking in a particular pub, but because the living *aren't* walking in the pub and trade is a bit slack. It's just another publicity stunt, like Santa Claus, the Bermuda Triangle, Bigfoot and time-travel: these are all things that people would like to believe in simply because everybody loves a good mystery; they make our dull lives that much more fun. But, alas, believing that something is so doesn't necessarily make it so.

12) Any union member who does not wish to join in a

strike, but is nevertheless forced to do so for fear of being treated as a scab by his workmates, can register with his employers that he wishes to work but is unable to because of their heavy-handed petty-mindedness. As a result, he will receive 90% of his normal income throughout the course of the dispute, and be promoted to being their boss when they do finally condescend to return to work.

13) All international food-reserves – butter-mountains, wine-lakes, chocolate-pudding-ridges, marmalade-quarries and similar nonsenses, built up and stored solely for cold hard economic reasons, are to be dismantled at once and shipped off to feed the starving millions in developing countries, without any financial compensation whatsoever and without fretting too much about the consequences on the world economy.

14) Grants of public money to the arts, which are subsequently misused to produce ridiculous, self-indulgent non-artistic pieces of rubbish, are to be repaid by the artist within twenty-one days of the first complaint by a member of the public; and in addition, the morons who made the grant in the first place will be fined heavily, or else sentenced to a minimum of seven years' imprisonment for wasting taxpayers' money, with a further two years for insulting our intelligence.

The reason for this provision is self-evident. There is a point on the scale of human intellect, it seems, where people are so intelligent that they're stupid. And nowhere is this more evident than in the arts – whether we're talking sculpture, theatre, poetry, design, architecture, or whatever, the whole arty business is riddled with humourless trendies continually feeding their own self-serving fantasies and using *our* money to do it. Even they can barely believe that they've got away with it for so long.

Don't get me wrong. I'm not saying that people shouldn't be allowed to fritter away their own hard-earned cash in any way they choose. The New Right couldn't give a toss how an individual wastes his savings. But there comes a point where a potful of dahlias with the heads snapped off and called 'A Winter's Day in Aberystwyth' ceases to be 'sculpture', just as a large heap of dried dog-mess, painted silver, suspended three feet off the floor, and entitled 'Chaplin: a Tribute' is not an 'objet d'irt', it's a complete rip-off.

Therefore, everything from a bust of the Queen Mother done in meat-paste and firelighters, to a scale model of Copenhagen harbour fashioned in quark will be subjected to a merciless enquiry by a specially-formed Self-Indulgent Crap Detection Squad, and the culprits tracked down and taught the meaning of the word pain.

15) All drugs are to be legalised. In addition, health warnings will be removed from the side of cigarette packets and replaced with the words: '*The Health Experts screwed up* – smoking is great for you after all!'

This is an early imperative. For a start, promoting tobacco, particularly amongst the very young, will rake in huge quantities of revenue from taxation. This in turn will enable the government to plough money back into our public healthcare services, ready to treat the smokers later on when they have the inevitable strokes and heart-attacks in middle-age and become useless bedridden vegetables.

As with all drugs, hard or soft, one must preserve the freedom of the individual who wishes to take them. People should be free to kill themselves in any way they choose. But equally, those who do abuse their bodies in this or any other way, should be made wholly responsible for their stupidity and lack of foresight when they eventually fall ill. Therefore, all drug- and alcohol-dependency clinics will be closed forthwith and a sign hung on the door saying 'Told you so!'

16) Any political party opposed to the policies of The New Right will be robbed of their legal status within the parliamentary system and outlawed at once.

This is an excellent way to prevent your political bubble from bursting. You need to watch your back in this game – don't forget the old saying: 'What goes up must come down'. The only exceptions to this principle, it seems, are Phil Collins, the American flag and trains on the Northern Line. There is a natural ebb and flow to all political fortunes. All you have to do is make sure you flow far more than you ebb. This you can do successfully by banning the opposition.

17) All churches and religious denominations are to lose

their charitable status and will be obliged to publish accounts twice-yearly explaining where the hell all their money goes to.

18) Everyone else in the country is *to do as they're bloody well told!!*

Because the proposals laid out in The Bene Diktat are so fair, it makes sense that the country will vote for them almost as a matter of course, and put The New Right into power with a stonking great majority. Anything less would be unthinkable. And once we are in power, the measures listed above can be bulldozed through parliament in a matter of days.

Q: *I hate to say this, but I'm not convinced. It all sounds very extreme. I mean, what sort of government will The New Right be?*

I'll let Julie explain that.

'Fascist, probably – although I prefer the word "sensible".

'Let's face it, democracy sucks anyway, right? Based, as it is, on endless committee decisions and futile, long-winded debates – all that bullshit about 'agreeing to disagree' and so on. Pah! People don't want that. They want action and decisive government, not namby-pamby compromises all the

166

time. Clearly, what is called for is a dictatorship, a nice one, which is generous, just and open, caring, humane, bold, fearless and, above all, which takes no crap from anyone. That is what The New Right is all about.'

Q: *Oh*.

THE CABINET

Jeff and Julie are prepared to lead this country into a benevolent, fun-loving future. At the heart of their government will be a strong, honourable cabinet, with Jeff himself as Prime Minister and Mrs Greenhalgh bringing her robust but lovable West Country housekeeping approach to the Treasury. Vince 'Donkey-Dick' Osmond will be given a clean pair of trousers and a good wash and put in charge of the Foreign Office, Julie will maintain a watching brief in the Department of the Environment, and Lucette can expect to be promoted to Homo Secretary (with responsibility for overseeing the Police Force and Drugs Squad and granting official pardons to every member of Terror Firma who has committed an indictable offence during the execution of the World Domination Plan).

Last, and least, is the slightly trickier post of Secretary of State responsible for Northern Ireland. This job is frequently reserved for a politician who is either in disgrace or has blotted his copybook at some point in the past, or is generally disliked by every one of his colleagues.

Alas, Suzuki isn't old enough, otherwise she'd be ideal.

Without doubt, The New Right is a revolutionary breakthrough in world politics, true People Power, and should see families similar to the Abercorns taking to the stage in every country across the globe, uniting in their bid for world supremacy.

Jeff himself has already given his blessing to M. René Baldue, a French-speaking accountant, and his wife Renée, to take over Belgium, and to the van Rental family – Hertz and Avis van Rental and their children, Guy and Bødget, to do the same in Holland. The German end of things is in the

167

more-than-capable hands of Frau Barbara Ichblutebittever-bindenmich, and in Switzerland, Herr und Frau Stolle and their son Duane, have taken the helm.

A landslide in the general election at home, together with similar victories for The New Right in other democracies elsewhere, coupled with your efforts to unseat dictators around the world, should mean that you are now in a strong position to begin bargaining with the Superpowers on your own terms. The truth is, they simply can't ignore you: you're too big. Too many ordinary American and Russian citizens will, by now, be either devout believers in Faitheism or hopeless addicts of the Healthruherbs Compleat Health Plan. And above all else, you have too many Sainsbury's carrier-bags filled with plutonium-239 for your presence to go unnoticed.

And so, as Jeff and the rest of his newly-appointed cabinet celebrate their astounding, though hardly unexpected, victory from the top-deck of a round-Witchester sightseeing bus, he is fully aware that there is just one more stage to go before his plan is complete – the biggest, most challenging step of them all: the step to becoming World President.

7

Summit and Nothing

I bet, when you bought this book, you thought it was all a joke, right? That you would never in a million years, let alone one, get as far as actually taking over the country. Well, the promises we made at the start were all true, and now here you are, standing outside your new home – the official residence of the Prime Minister of Great Britain, about to become the very first President of the Whole World.

But once the novelty of being so powerful has worn off, you will find that there is a downside to being the figurehead of a nation. In fact, there are four very major downsides, and you ought to be aware of them before you go much further.

NO 1. YOU'LL HAVE VAST QUANTITIES OF MONEY

That's right. Assuming that you've been following these instructions closely, you will doubtless have stacks of money by now – maybe even *stacks* and stacks, who knows? – and be wondering what the hell you're going to do with it all.

I. What to do with it

Jeff has his own ideas, of course.

Being a down-to-earth kind of fella not prone to needless extravagance, he has decided to play safe and stash most of the profits from The Most Unholy Church of St Thomas the Doubter and Healthruherbs plc, totalling well over £417 million, in his own secret numbered bank account in Vienna. This is sound advice as a matter of fact, and you would be wise to follow suit when dividing up the spoils of your own little venture.

170

Then take whatever is left over and invest it in a few simple luxuries for your family: don't feel guilty about this, you've earned it. And the curious thing is that, the richer you become and the more sickeningly gaudy your lifestyle, the more your followers will love you for it.

We noted earlier the perverse nature of religious converts, who willingly hand over huge slices of their quite meagre income to people they have never met, in the baffling and wholly groundless belief that this will guarantee them a passport to Heaven when the times comes. Many television evangelists in the United States exploit this gullibility to the limit and enjoy mind-bogglingly luxurious lifestyles as a result. In fact, most of them can't believe how foolish their congregations are. You don't question it, though, you just keep on preaching and raking in the money, and worry about getting found out when it actually happens.

II. What else to do with it
One item you won't be able to do without is a satellite TV station.

The Abercorns plan to set up their own non-religious satellite channel, called AFT – Agnostic Fundamentalist Television, modelled closely on the Christian cable networks in America, and intended to reach out to Faitheists, Doubters, Malcontents and Bored-Again Christians everywhere.

AFT will serve a number of purposes. It will be:

i) a round-the-clock begging bowl, inducing its followers to donate more money than they can afford, by offering them forgiveness, love, everlasting life and a host of other rash and impossible-to-keep promises:

ii) an invisible hand of comfort, love and friendship stretching out through the TV screen, converting foolhardy viewers to the spiritually vacuous wonders of Faitheism; and finally,

iii) a global boutique of the air, flogging millions of pounds worth of the tattiest merchandise imaginable, every last piece of which is a religious icon – with the emphasis on the 'con'. This merchandise will only be available through AFT, simply because nobody else could hope to sell such rubbish and get away with it.

Products include a range of ceramic T-shirts, all bearing the Faitheist motif and cute, eye-catching messages such as 'There's No-One Up There, You're On Your Own' and 'Faitheism is a blast for me'; and an attractively overpriced video called 'Purgatory Hour': '. . . forty minutes of homespun fireside entertainment in the company of Jeff and Julie Abercorn, in which they openly discuss the non-existence of an external God-force with their dear friends Bobby Womack, Pee Wee Herman and D-I-Y expert Barry Bucknall. Plus, there's a surprise appearance from their special singing guest, Col. Oliver North. The video also features never-before-seen shots of snooker-player Hurricane Higgins prior to his death. (It may be a while yet, but when he finally does die, these shots will be priceless, just you watch!)'

III. Yet more things to do with it

Besides serving its purpose as a mainstream communications facility, the AFT satellite is to be equipped with a gigantic concave mirror attached to the outside, which will be positioned in geo-stationary orbit 1,500 miles above Great Britain.

The idea is that it will catch rays directly from the sun and concentrate them, using several dozen tiny angled reflectors, into a single beam of light, which can then be focused onto any part of the earth that Jeff chooses, wreaking untold global devastation. It would wipe out tiny villages in no time, or whole cities, or even gigantic slices of any country whose leaders did not consent to the Abercorns becoming world supremos.[7]

Brilliant!

The next consequence of being Prime Minister is:

[7] A word of caution, though: if you do decide to follow Jeff's example and place an order for one of these multi-faceted reflector attachments for your satellite, be sure to explain to the representative from British Aerospace that the device is to be used for peaceful purposes only, and not for any sinister military gain; otherwise The Men In Grey Suits could get mighty suspicious and descend on you like a ton of pricks!

172

NO 2. YOU'LL BE RECOGNISED EVERYWHERE YOU GO

True.

a) You will be pestered constantly by *Acolytes*: wild-eyed fawning hangers-on who worship the water you walk on and insist on christening their first-born child after you.

This happens time and again with top people. Wave after wave of Traceys and Matts and Cashes and Ringos and so on will usually follow in the wake of one particularly celebrity called Tracey or Matt or Cash or Ringo. In fact, I wonder how many parents now regret calling their new-born son Sting or Yahoo, and how many young Sinittas, Limahls, Yazzes, Bonios, Enyas and Kylies will be queuing up in twenty years' time to change their name to plain old Margaret, Harold, Judith or Carol.

But that's not all. You will also find yourself being showered with unwanted and quite undeserved accolades.

Entire shopping-malls will be named after you, not to mention ocean-going liners, public parks and golf-courses in any one of a thousand locations from Yamaha, Nebraska, to Wurlitzer, Oregon. Before long, you'll be a patron of the Tate Gallery, with your own wing housing the world's largest collection of Money-Off coupons – some in protective cases, others underwater; together with a fascinating display of Sheena Easton's worst press-clippings and an exhibition tracing the design of the New Brighton Ferry Timetable from 1958 to the present day.

You will receive a flood of invitations to give lectures, write books, lay foundation stones, plant trees, become Dr Who's next assistant, play guest piano on Phil Collins' latest album, unveil the plaque at a new dental hospital . . . the opportunities for showing off are endless.

My tip: avoid them all! True posterity comes only to those who try and dodge it. Remember what Andy Warhol said: 'Someday, famous people will quote me every fifteen minutes.' And he was right.

b) The second pack of freaks on your tail will be the *Snipers*.

The moment you come out of the closet and make a stand

for something you believe in, no matter how mundane that 'something' may be, scores of critics seem to emerge suddenly from a different closet to take a stand against you – not because they oppose you necessarily, but simply because they lead empty lives themselves and it gives them something to do.

These are the chaps who send anonymous death-threats to public figures, threats which they have no intention of carrying out, but which they know will strike terror into the heart of their victims. And they are the ones who, the moment they discover the address of somebody famous, will rush round at the dead of night to push shit through his letterbox.

They like nothing more than to create an almighty stink about plans to build a new by-pass, or the volume of aircraft-noise above their homes, or some factory being constructed on a field colonised by badgers, etc etc. They are – and this is viewing them in the rosiest, most pleasant, unprejudiced light possible – complete bastards. Cross them, and they'll have your testicles for cake-decorations! So steer well clear, okay?

A further, more substantial, consequence of being in charge of a country is:

NO. 3. OTHER WORLD LEADERS WILL KEEP INVITING YOU TO SUMMIT MEETINGS

Sounds like a drag, doesn't it? But don't be put off by the title.

A summit is just the official name given to a social occasion in which senior politicians drink a lot of sherry, have their picture taken together as a group, and proclaim that everything, just everything, is hunky-dory with the whole world. They are lying and everyone knows it, but that's all part of the fun.

For good measure, when the leaders emerge into the glare of the TV lights, they will usually add that the meeting has gone terribly well and that both sides have enjoyed a 'meaningful dialogue'. (Meaningful dialogue is official jargon for 'we seemed to drink a lot of sherry, but otherwise didn't achieve very much'; whereas if they say, 'we had a full and frank discussion', that means 'we argued the whole time until the other side stormed out in protest and buggered up the whole day!')

For Jeff, though, it is far more than just a social chat. To

174

him, a summit is his big chance to confront the Presidents of the United States and the USSR, whom, for the sake of argument, we'll call George Bush and Mikhail Gorbachev, and induce them to sign a formal treaty appointing Jeff as Global President.

a) Location

To avoid the usual torrent of journalistic interest, the summit should be held secretly, in some mutually agreed location which members of the press will not wish to visit: somewhere where the water is undrinkable, the food is disgusting, the hotels, houses and streets look dirty and uncared for. Not an easy decision to make, but with the help of Julie and Mrs Greenhalgh, Jeff has managed to draw up a shortlist of possible locations which fit the bill exactly. These are as follows:

i) France.

. . . and more precisely the market-town of St Quentin, which is only thirteen miles from Montelimar Centre.

b) The Talks

By all means check it out for yourself, but you can take my word for it that St Quentin is ideal for a high-powered, low-profile, medium-range but far-reaching conference of this sort: an average sort of town, full of overpriced bread-shops, bars and restaurants, with a large, traffic-jam at its centre and lots of smaller traffic jams spiralling out from it into the suburbs.

The talks are to be held at Le Cafe de la Pustule, Place de l'Hotel de Ville, St Quentin (Tel: Maxime 03.662.76.5811. 20% reductions for coachparties, group bookings and top-level presidential discussions). It's a comfortable, no-frills bistro, intimate enough to lend a certain *je-sais-exactement-quoi* to the talks themselves, yet large enough to make the hiring of it a complete waste of French tax-payers' money.

Jeff has rehearsed his lines carefully, running through the exact words he will say to Bush and Gorbachev as they sit huddled around the table, nibbling at toasted cheese sand-wiches and sipping capuccino that tastes like Daz Liquid. The deal, put simply, amounts to this:

'Right, listen to me, you bastards! I have a powerful solar reflector floating in space right now, and it's trained directly on Moscow and Washington. One word from me, and bloody millions of your people will be burned alive, okay? So sign this treaty appointing me World President or I'll blow both your countries out of the fuckin' water!

'. . . Now, does anyone have a pen?'

That should do it, I think: tough and uncompromising with just the right number of swearwords to convey heartfelt sincerity without causing unnecessary offence.

Minutes later, all three parties will emerge from the cafe to pose for a photo-opportunity, smiling and shaking hands and declaring it to have been 'a full and frank discussion.' They may hate the tight corner you have driven them into, yet will see that they have no choice but to concede defeat and let you have what you want.

This is one possible outcome of the summit talks. But equally, there is another result which can't be wholly discounted, and it also happens to be the fourth in our list of consequences which follow when you become a world leader.

NO 4. YOU'LL BE SHOT DEAD

Remember in Chapter 5, when we discussed the different kinds of Unpleasantness that The Men In Grey Suits may try and inflict upon you the moment you show signs of upsetting the status quo? And remember I said that there was one kind which promised to be the worst of the lot, the ultimate act of meanness, one they would only resort to in the most extreme circumstances?

Well, here it is!

For men as powerful and distinguished as Bush and Gorbachev, circumstances don't come more extreme than some complete stranger turning up from nowhere and turfing them out of office. Nobody has ever had George Bush over a barrel – not even Barbara Bush, I should think! – and so it's almost a dead cert that you will now encounter this, the ultimate act of meanness: *assassination!*

You mustn't take an assassination attempt too personally, however. Or as some kind of slight on your character. That's not the intention at all. In fact, it is more like a pat on the back from the authorities, a sign that you have made your mark at last by becoming so popular and so respected by so many godzillions of decent honest people everywhere, that you must now be disposed of quickly and quietly before things get out of hand. Indeed, it's as if there exists in life a certain threshold of popularity: go beyond it, and you will not only be canonised, you'll probably be Lennonised as well!

Q: *Oh shit!! You didn't tell me about this when we started out.*

177

Who's going to try and kill me? Who will pull the trigger –
The Men In Grey Suits?

No fear! They will be nowhere in sight, you can be sure of that.

The job will be assigned to a scapegoat, some crackpot with a Baryshnikov rifle who, in spite of rigorous security checks, will have managed to weasel himself into a vantage point overlooking La Place de L'Hotel de Ville, ready to take potshots at your motorcade as it leaves the summit. He is just a stooge planted by The Men In Grey Suits, a psycho who has been thoroughly brainwashed until his only purpose in life is to stalk you, track you down and blast your brains out. He won't know why, he will just have this overwhelming urge to spend thirty years in prison for homicide.

Q: *Oh, well that's just great, isn't it? I come all this way, I slog my guts out. I start religions and health-food companies . . . and now you say I'm going to die. Christ, I'm not bloody Jane Fonda! Is there **nothing** I can do to get out of this mess?*

Of course there is . . . Jane Fonda?

Q: *Sorry, Martin Luther King.*

Right. If that's the way you feel about it, and you want to end the game here, my advice is to do precisely what Jeff himself has done. On the way to the summit talks, he makes a quick call to Jeff Jnr back at The Badger's Rectum, and asks him to read out this week's forecast by Kosmik Kirsty in The Witchester Echo. It runs like this:

Gemini: Not the best week for entering into arguments, so try to keep a low profile at work. A chance encounter with a stranger mid-week could affect your life for months or even years to come, especially if he is carrying a pump-action shotgun and is positioned at a third floor window in the building opposite. Mars is currently in Virgo, so watch your step, otherwise you could end up with three bullets in the back of the head.

Three bullets??

Three is Jeff's lucky number!

Uncanny.

Still, he is not about to throw himself on the mercy of some crazed, sack-o'-shit assassin in the secret pay of The Men In Grey Suits.

Obviously, it is time to call it a day, to quit the operation and go back to leading an ordinary life, content in the knowledge that at least he made it this far, putting the wind up a few complacent churchmen, bucking the System, upsetting the status quo and making stacks and stacks of money along the way; money which is, right this minute, sitting there in his account in Austria begging to be frittered away on Rolls-Royce Silver Shadows and a hundred other mindless luxuries.

So if you find yourself in his position, don't waste another moment. Grab your things and scarper, that's what I say! For the last time, think of The Movie. When your story of heroism, courage and driving persistence against overwhelming odds is made into a motion picture, you want to be at the premiere, not stuck underground in a box discovering that you were wrong and that there is a Hell after all!

It's your decision: how do you want the story to end?

Like something by Alan Parker maybe? . . . Shot in sombre black and white with broody pensive synthesiser music rumbling in the background, as the camera tracks slowly across your bullet-ravaged body slumped lifeless at the table in Le Cafe de la Pustule, the back of your head blown away, an arm missing, blood coursing down onto the gingham cloth from the corner of your mouth . . .

The fan on the ceiling beats the air – sshrikk-sshrikk-sshrikkk, swirling indifferently over the mountain of twisted bodies – waiters, private detectives and *Daily Mail* photographers . . . Somewhere upstairs, Mickey Rourke is humping away with a second-rate actress just out of drama-school, their rhythmic heaving and panting only faintly audible over the soundtrack music and the first wail of sirens as half a dozen police-cars and ambulances weave painstakingly into shot through the traffic in rue Gavinessler and on towards La Place De L'Hotel de Ville . . .

179

Well?

Is that how you see it ending? In death, silence, lakes of blood, a brief shot of Mickey Rourke slipping back into his 501s before he staggers down the stairs and out into the backstreets, followed by a slow fade to black and then a long, weary credit-roll as cinema-goers reach for their coats and bags and file off noisily towards the exits? Is it?

Or might you have something else in mind? A sequel perhaps – '*World Domination II: Okay, We Made A Complete Hash Of It The First Time Round, So Let's Have Another Go*', in which you live to fight another day . . .? Because if that is the case, then you had better do something about it fast. Make sure you leave the audience laughing and wanting more.

The Closing Sequence

Here we go, then, with the Presidential Summit Take Two, only this time we will make sure it has a positive, uplifting, wholesome, jolly ending – so let's hope that Alan Parker's busy and Spielberg buys the film rights!

b) The Talks

Presidents Bush and Gorbachev arrive at the cafe, and Jeff as Prime Minister of Great Britain greets them warmly, ordering cheese on toast for three and threatening both of them with untold annihilation from his solar reflector if they don't sign the treaty. Of course, there is no question of a refusal, and they agree to it without reservation, endorsing Jeff's immediate accession to the World Presidency at long last.

Hurrah!

Within minutes, the three men emerge from Le Cafe de la Pustule smiling and shaking hands. Jeff waves the signed treaty at the hushed crowd and they erupt into a cacophany of cheers and praise for their new leader, shaking flags and chair-legs and singing at the top of their voices.

'Strike up the band, maestro!' cries Jeff, beaming victoriously. 'Let's have a French celebration – Hollywood-style.'

180

With that, he turns to Julie and gives her one of those maddeningly overlong soft-focus movie kisses. 'We did it, babe,' he says, hugging her close to his chest and wiping a rogue tear from her cheek with his thumb.

'Oh, I do so love you, Jeff,' whispers Julie, running her fingers back and forth through his thick, manly thatch.

Jeff steps back for a second, then smiles broadly and gives his wife another tight hug. 'Just call me . . . Mr President.'

Hurrah!!!

From out of nowhere comes a parade of dancers in glittering top hats and tails, with beautiful girls twirling parasols and ranks of cockney knife-grinders and flower-sellers high-kicking their way in amongst the cars in rough unison. A bevy of drunks from the nearby tavern unite in toasting Jeff's good health and long success, whilst several local attorneys cavort around the car-park in a frenzied devilish carousel (I'm not sure what the collective noun for such professional people is, to tell you the truth, although 'a thick brown stain of attorneys' seems rather appropriate, don't you think?). And all the while, hundreds of curious bystanders look on as the KGB and CIA agents sway energetically to the infectious swing of the music, in a blizzard of marigold leaves and sea-urchins blown across the square in the bright mid-morning sunshine.

'If I ruled the world,' sings Jeff.
'Every day would be the first day of spring,
Every heart would have a new song to sing,
And we'd sing
Of the joy a new morning would bring.

If I ruled the world . . .'

Yes, well, you get the picture anyway.

This is how crooner Harry Secombe, the patron saint of global revolution, put it in song twenty years ago – though, frankly, if you do become World President, you are hopefully going to do a little more than make every day the first day of spring, right? You will be introducing monumental changes that are long overdue and which should have been made decades ago, only nobody had the guts to do it.

So, come on, everyone, let's hear it for the Abercorns and the success of their World Domination Plan! Join together with us in a sickly singalong number that will wind up side two of the soundtrack album, and which looks set to ruin what was otherwise a perfectly acceptable finale.

Chorus of KGB agents: Mmmmm. Mmmmm.
The way we all abuse the earth
Is an abomination,
So tip your hat and shout three cheers,
For Global Domination!

Julie: From now on, there'll be . . .

Company: . . . shelter for the homeless, treatment for the sick
And every OAP will get a walking frame or stick.
We're banning zoos and circuses and putting stop to war,
And making sure that famines never happen any more.

Jeff: We've hostages to liberate and prisoners to free.
Let's round up any fake Messiahs and nail them to a tree.

Lucette: We'll suffocate apartheid and stamp out acid rain,
And make damned sure that Bonnie Langford never sings again.

Jeff Jnr: If teenagers are hooked on smack,
We'll try to wean them off it;

Mrs Greenhalgh: And make McDonald's tell us
What they do with all their profit!

Suzuki: We'll b . . . OWW!!

Mrs Greenhalgh: Shut up, yer little bugger. Nobody said you could sing!

182

CIA operatives:	Mmmmmmmm-aaaaaaaahhhhhh! Mmmmmmmm-aaaaaaaahhhhhh!

Save the ozone,
Cleanse the seas,
Tell Brazil
To plant more trees . . .
    Ban fur coats
    And ivoreee
    No more nuclear
    Energeee . . .
        Wave goodbye
        To human bonds,
        Hatred, fear,
        And atom bombs . . .

. . . Flags are waved, trumpets blare, tickertape rains down and the jubilant crowd throws confetti and cans of grapefruit segments at the passing parade . . .

Finally, as the dancing rises to a frantic crescendo with a couple of psychopathic snipers being arrested by laughing FBI men, and all fanatical Muslim death squads in the area being gamely rounded up and given a sound ticking off; and as two dozen grinning showgirls plant full cherry kisses onto an enlarged colour photograph of Colonel Gadaffi . . . through a veil of rose-petals emerges a mystery figure, dressed in a velvet tunic, a bright red flowing cape and a wide-brimmed hat shadowing his face.

Who can it be?

It can't be Mickey Rourke, he wouldn't be seen dead in a cape! So who *is* this enigmatic stranger?

The whole square falls silent whilst the Mystery Man walks forward and steps onto a podium. All eyes are fixed on him. Small children are hoisted up onto their father's shoulders for a better view. He pauses for a second or two, then raises a hand to his hat, takes hold of the brim and slowly, very slowly, pulls it away from his head . . . to reveal . . .

MR CARMICHAEL, the tramp from the precinct!!

The smile quickly drops away from Jeff's lips, as the crowds erupt into cheers once more and begin to sing in unison.

Full Company: So as Democrats shout 'Scandal!'
And Republicans cry 'Shame!'
We may be down at half-time,
But we'll surge to win the game.

To fighting, famine, drought, disease,
We give our condemnations,
Cos as Jeff sez – and he's the Pres –
We're all United Nations!

ROLL END CREDITS

Bbbrrriiiiinnnngggg! Bbbrrriiiiinnnngggg!

8

Let's Wave Goodbye to the Abercorns

Bbbrrriiiiinnnngggg! Bbbrrriiiiinnnngggg!

In World Domination circles there is a little something we call 'The Mary Poppins Principle'. Ask anybody who has ever tried to conquer the entire planet and they'll know what I'm talking about.

It can be summed up very quickly as follows: do as much as you can, go as far as you can and win the game as often as you can, but when the wind changes, get out as fast as you can. In other words, the moment you feel your luck running out, run out after it. Total success is never guaranteed when you are playing for such high stakes and you can't sod around waiting for a miracle to happen. Be prepared to season the simmering hotpot of your revolutionary fervour with a few fresh herbs of common sense, as Mrs Greenhalgh might say . . .

Bbbrrriiiiinnnngggg! Bbbrrriiiiinnnngggg!

Q: *Excuse me. There appears to be a telephone ringing*

Hush!

. . . And that is why Mr World President Jeff Abercorn is taking the First Lady of Earth, Julie, and the rest of his family over the mountains into Austria, where they will be safe from The Men In Grey Suits, and free to enjoy a fabulous luxurious lifestyle well away from the jealous eyes of all those poor gullible idiots who gave them the money in the first place.

If you followed their instructions to the letter, you are no doubt not too far behind them. On the other hand, if you are still in two minds about it, and unsure whether you really have what it takes to be the new Jeff or Julie Abercorn, then just

185

remember this: when the next war comes, it won't be 'Russia *v* America' or 'Libya *v* Britain', or any of the conflicts you've been warned about. It will be a long, drawn-out, bloody battle between ordinary people and the faceless bureaucrats who try to exert control over every little aspect of our lives. Moreover, the side that will win is the side which controls the strongest, most powerful weapon ever invented by mankind: The Media.

Brrrrrrrrrriiiiinnnnnggggg!! Brrrrrrrrrriiiiinnnnnggggg!!

Q: *Look, is somebody going to get that?*

The saddest part, though, is that ordinary people would never dare do anything on their own – they're sheep! They will just sit back and expect to be told what to do by someone who is strong enough to lead them, someone who knows The Truth About Everything and understands what The Men In Grey Suits are up to.

So when war finally does break out, who will take up the challenge and spearhead this revolt against the System?

Will it be you?

Brrrrrrrrrrriiiiiiiiiiiinnnnnnnnnnnnggggggggg!!

Q: *The bloody phone's ringing – it could be for one of the readers!*

Oh . . . hell's bells!!

Hang on, I'll get it . . .

Hello? . . . Yes, Operator, I'll pay for the call . . . Hello? Oh, hi there! Fine . . . yes, okay . . . yes . . .

Great. Sounds wonderful . . . I don't know what they'll say actually. Sure, hold it right there, Stevie baby, I'll ask.

It's Steven Spielberg on the line from Hollywood. He says he wants to turn your life-story into a movie.

What shall I tell him?

ten	knave	queen	king	ace
over	past	dead	gone	Tutte
hand	ankle	wrist	foot	the
Ladies'	Circle	count	to	frog
seek	note	search	find	Daz
watch	time	I'm	it	donkey
false	iffy	correct	lies	true
parcel	sheet	letter	page	m.way
then	all	was	merry	yule
eight	one-	twelve	nine	seven
see	read	write	Soldiers	stone
u.pass	compass	hammer	spade	Jason
50	7/1/89	98.5	1/1-2	6/6-6
feel	suspect	know	sense	damson
through	mind	begin:	by	jam
then	this	that	those	Soldiers
Norfolk	Hampshire	Cheshire	Yorkshire	Cornwall
peril	nasty	danger	fear	eat
should	if	when	whether	g.luck

1	1	20	13	19	83	5	6	31	42
28	15	1	1	11	13	6	1	68	26
9	21	14	1	8	3	42	26	2	18
4	27	7	40	3	8	7	66	20	2
74	5	3	4	21	13	7	1	1	13
M	2	7	1	2	1	6	2	0	1
23	5	2	15	26	13	6	7	4	28
1	29	7	2	9	1	15	2	14	6

Grateful thanks are extended to the following people:

Lt Donald Barron and Col. Hoffman of the Reserve Officer Training Corps, US Army, Las Cruces, New Mexico; Sgt Pete Swinge of PT7, The Metropolitan Police Firearms Unit, London; Sgt-Major Andy Warner and the lads of 7 Para, The Parachute Regiment, Aldershot; the Security Staff at the White Sands Missile Range, New Mexico; Richard Jones and Geoffrey Pimm of The Lord Chancellor's Department, London.

Paul McKenna – master hypnotist;
Anthony Timpson – computer maverick;
Ian Hardy – radio ham.

John Barbat, Erin Barron, James Ricketts, Andrew Irving, Ian Duncan, Tim Moat, James RQ Pinder, Max Ellis, Jacqui Deevoy, Adrian Nicholas, Carl Adams, Rory Bridson, Andrew Pooley, Bill Steinburg and Loveday Miller.

. . . without whom this page would have been completely blank.